DISCOVER
DECOUPAGE

DISCOVER
DECOUPAGE

40 ORIGINAL PROJECTS TO
BUILD YOUR PAPERCRAFT SKILLS

MAGGIE PHILO

hamlyn

First published in Great Britain in 1994 by Hamlyn
an imprint of Octopus Publishing Group Limited
2–4 Heron Quays, London E14 4JP
Reprinted 1995,1996
First published in paperback in 1999

©**OCTOPUS PUBLISHING GROUP LIMITED** 1994

Distributed in the United States
by Sterling Publishing Co., Inc.
387 Park Avenue South, New York, NY100016-8810

SERIES EDITOR: **JONATHAN HILTON**
SERIES ART EDITOR: **PRUE BUCKNELL**
ART EDITOR: **ALISON SHACKLETON**
EXECUTIVE EDITOR: **JUDITH MORE**
ART DIRECTOR: **JACQUI SMALL**

PHOTOGRAPHS BY: **LUCY MASON**

The publishers have made every effort to ensure that all instructions
given in this book are accurate and safe, but they cannot accept liability
for any resulting injury, damage or loss to either person or property
whether direct or consequential and howsoever arising. The author and
publishers will be grateful for any information which will assist them in
keeping future editions up to date.

ISBN: 0 600 59949 3

DTP ALISON SHACKLETON
PRODUCED BY TOPPAN PRINTING CO LTD
PRINTED AND BOUND IN HONG KONG

CONTENTS

INTRODUCTION

Découpage is the craft of decorating the surfaces of objects with cut-outs of printed images. The piece is then given numerous layers of varnish to protect and to conceal the edges of the paper, producing the impression that the design has been hand painted or is somehow an integral part of that object's surface.

When I first started teaching découpage there was very little published on the subject, except for Hiram Manning's wonderful book *Manning on Découpage*. Since then, however, there have been many advances in the formulae used for paints and varnishes and, having largely forsaken oil-based products for environmentrally and user friendly water-based ones, I began to experiment with different glues, varnishes and paints. The first piece I produced was a galvanized bucket, decorated with a giftwrap of a Dutch flower painting. Using water-based mediums throughout, it all worked perfectly. "This isn't so tricky – no problems teaching this," I thought. It wasn't long, however, before the students started showing me the horrible things that could indeed go wrong – all those bubbles, tears and crinkles! Having gone on to produce work for sale, and having taught dozens of students, I can usually salvage all but the most catastrophic of mistakes and – more importantly – prevent most of them from happening.

I now find découpage a wonderfully rewarding subject to teach. It is good to see people who arrive at a class, perhaps a little nervous and unsure, showing such excitement as their work progresses. There are so many wonderful styles to draw on that, almost without exception, students will leave a course with a design they are happy with.

Another bonus for the découpage enthusiast is that it does not cost a lot to get started. There is no expensive kit to buy, although a good-quality pair of manicure scissors is essential. You will often be able to find objects to work on in your home or garden, or items can be bough inexpensively at junk shops; designs can be taken from magazines, giftwraps or photocopies from books, postcards and prints. The biggest expense will probably be the amount of varnish you need. But don't be put off – if you are happy with your results after three or four coats, then fine. All the pieces in this book, however, received at least ten coats. While the care taken in cutting out and the overall finish are important, a good combination of colour and design and the overall balance of an arrangement in relation to the size and shape of the item being worked on mean more to me than not being able to feel the raised surface of the paper under the varnish. I should also mention the therapeutic value of découpage. It can be very relaxing to sit down and cut out while listening to your favourite music. This pleasure now eludes me since I have an absolutely amazing mother who does virtually all my cutting out while I frantically paint, glue and varnish to keep up with my commissioned work. However, I did do most of the cutting out for this book, so I am not completely out of practice!

This book has allowed me to experiment with different styles of découpage and I can't wait to start using some of the wonderful papers I came across. These have now been added to my huge library of images – I have a compulsive urge to visit every bargain book store I pass. I hope you will be stimulated by some of the following projects and that you will be able to interpret these to transform everyday items into beautiful objects you will enjoy and cherish.

A BRIEF HISTORY

Découpage as we know it today first became popular in Venice during the 18th century, when there was an enormous demand for painted furniture. In order to supply the quantity required, craftsmen would mass produce prints of their original designs, which were then hand coloured by their young apprentices. The popularity of this style of furniture spread to France and it wasn't long before it was taken up by the ladies of the French court. They cut and then pasted prints, specifically reproduced for the purpose, on to boxes, fans, screens and other furniture. Upward of 30 coats of varnish were then applied so that the finished piece resembled the oriental lacquer work that was so fashionable during this period.

The work of many famous artists of the time was used, and their prints were reproduced in *Ladies Amusement*, a book published in 1762. Among the most popular were the prints of Pillement, with his enchanting chinoiserie imagery, and Boucher, who had a more romantic, rococo style.

During the 19th century the process of chromolithography was invented and coloured embossed prints and scraps made their first appearance. Romantic and sentimental themes of angelic children, well-dressed fashionable ladies, flowers, angels and fans replaced the chinoiserie favoured by practitioners of the previous century. Folding and fire screens, boxes and trunks were popular choices for decoration and often the entire surface would be covered with randomly arranged, overlapping scraps.

Découpage went into decline at the turn of this century, but never quite died. A well-known 20th-century practitioner was a Mrs Delaney, who, at the age of 72, introduced a radically new style. She created amazingly accurate flower pictures by mounting layer upon layer of tissue paper, which she often coloured by hand and arranged on a black background. Her work can still be seen today in the British Museum. It was inevitable, however, with the interest in traditional painted finishes in recent years and the current vogue for painted furniture, that découpage would make a comeback. It is hard to understand why, after more than two centuries of popularity, it ever lost favour. The Victorian scraps are still available, as are designs similar to those used in the 18th century. Additionally we now have a vast choice of giftwraps and the advantage of photocopiers to extend the creative possibilities and, once again, we are snipping a pasting.

MATERIALS AND TECHNIQUES

One of the most satisfying aspects of découpage is transforming ordinary household items of no real value into stunning works of art. You will probably find that there are many things around your own home that, with the help of découpage, could be given a new lease of life. Old biscuit tins, tea caddies and baby-milk tins are all excellent items on which to practice and will make pretty storage containers for the kitchen. Junk shops provide all sorts of wonderful and interesting objects, too, such as old enamel jugs, bread bins and even bedpans!

The condition of these things does not really matter all that much, nor whether or not they are practical – it is what you do to them that is important. If you are lucky, you may find interesting old wooden boxes, a butler's tray or small pieces of furniture. Once découpaged, old trunks can look stunning, as can violin cases. These items can often be bought for next to nothing and they can end up looking like treasured antiques. Other sources of small wooden boxes and chests are craft supply shops and you will sometimes find hat boxes advertised for

sale in the back of women's magazines. Don't forget to look in your local hardware store for galvanized buckets, watering cans and coal scuttles – they will be scarcely recognizable once you have given them a few coats of paint and added some appropriate motifs. As you will see in this book, almost any hard surface is suitable for découpage, including glass, smooth terracotta and cardboard.

PRIMING AND PREPARING DIFFERENT SURFACES

For most people, this is the least favourite part of the procedure, but it is almost always necessary. The surfaces to which you apply your cut-out motifs must be prepared with fastidious care, especially if there are any signs of rust on metal objects or holes, cracks or splits in wooden ones.

NEW WOOD
Either seal new wood with a quick-drying, water-based undercoat or primer or, if you want to maintain the natural colour and

TIPS

● Before starting work on an old piece thoroughly clean it with detergent and water to remove all traces of dirt and grease.

● Fill cracks, holes or splits and sand back to leave a smooth, even surface.

● New pieces often need sanding back to provide a key that allows the primer to cover properly.

● Always check that you use the appropriate type of primer for the object being worked on.

grain of the wood, with a coat of shellac sanding sealer. If you wish, use a dark shellac to take away its "new" appearance. When the wood is dry, lightly sand it to provide a key for the adhesive to stick to.

OLD WOOD

With wood that has been painted or varnished, first wipe it over with detergent and water and then fill any holes, splits or cracks with wood filler. Next, sand the surface with a medium-grit sandpaper, ensuring that the surface of the filler is flush with the wood. Then use undercoat or primer, or leave it to be painted later.

NEW GALVANIZED METAL

The first step is to washed the object inside and out with detergent and water to remove its greasy surface and then paint it with galvanized metal primer to provide a key for painting. This liquid turns the metal black as it dries and, when it is dry, rinse it off with clean water. The object is then ready for painting.

WEATHERED GALVANIZED METAL

Weathered galvanized metal needs no special preparation, apart from cleaning with water. If, however, there are signs of rust,

follow the advice below for dealing with rusting and old metal.

RUSTING AND OLD METAL

Unless treated, the rust on metal will eventually eat through the paint and spoil your work. First, remove flaking and loose metal with a wire brush or coarse sandpaper. Then either treat it with a rustproofing agent and paint it with oil-based primer or use two coats of an all-in-one rust proofer and primer.

NEW TIN AND ENAMEL

Water-based paints do not adhere well to tin or enamel, so you will first need to paint them with an oil-based metal primer, one coat is usually sufficient.

TERRACOTTA

Terracotta pots, plaques and other objects can make ideal surfaces on which to work. Preparation is not usually difficult. First, sand the surface of any new terracotta object lightly and, second, seal it with a single coat of water-based varnish. If you are thinking of using an old or a used terracotta pot, you will first have to clean it thoroughly to remove any old soil or raised areas of lime scale.

PAPER RESOURCES

The choice of papers from which to take motifs is huge. But you can never have too many designs on hand, so save anything you come across until you find the right object to use it on.

GIFT WRAPPINGS AND BOOKS

There are many gift wrappings suitable for découpage. Good places to look include museums, galleries, book shops and large department stores. You will not find many modern designs used in this book, however, because of copyright conditions. But there is nothing to stop you using some of them yourself providing that you do not gain commercially from them.

Images from books can be used with great success and they provide an infinite variety of subjects. If you find the idea of cutting up a book inhibiting, even one bought inexpensively at a discount shop, you can always take a photocopy.

VICTORIAN SCRAPS AND PRINTS

The wonderfully evocative Victorian scrap images that were so popular in the last century are still produced today, and they remain virtually unchanged. These scraps are easily obtainable by mail order if you have difficulty finding them locally.

Traditionally, black and white prints, often coloured by hand, were used for découpage. Today we can take photocopies from books, prints and photographs, without spoiling the original. Photocopies can also be enlarged or reduced to fit the piece being worked on.

OTHER SOURCES

You can use images from magazines, but not newspapers since the print on the back is likely to show through. Postcards can also be used, but you will need to thin the card by putting your thumbnail between the layers of the image and the backing sheet and peeling them apart. If the image layer is in danger of tearing, start again from another corner. Highly glossy cards have a tendency to curl once thinned, which makes gluing a little more tricky, but otherwise they are fine to use.

TINTING AND COLOURING PRINTS

The simplest and most effective way of tinting a photocopy is to stain the paper with a wet tea bag. This takes away the harsh whiteness of the paper and gives it more the look of old parchment. Simply put a tea bag in a cup with about ½in (1.5cm) of boiling water to make a fairly strong brew. When this has cooled, wipe the surface of the paper with the tea bag and leave it to dry. You could experiment on a spare piece of paper, perhaps adding a little more water or giving it a second coating with the tea bag after the first has dried, until you get the colour required.

If you want a coloured print, coloured pencils and watercolour paints are the easiest to use. If you have not tried these mediums before, don't be daunted by the thought. Take a few extra copies of your chosen print and practise on these spares first, using perhaps just two or three colours or tones of the same colour. You don't even have to worry about smudging the edges because you are going to cut round them later. The black and white prints have shaded and light areas to guide you, and all you need to do is to start with the lightest tones and gradually build up the stronger or darker colours in the darkest areas. If you like, you can leave the very lightest areas white

COLOURED PENCILS

When you are using coloured pencils, make a series of light strokes next to each other, running in the same direction as those on the print. Gradually build these up to produce the colour density you require, rather than randomly filling in an area in the way a child would do. You can then work a beige-coloured pencil over the surface to blend the whole together.

WATERCOLOURS

If you use watercolours – an inexpensive box of student's colours is all you need – build up layers of colour, leaving the paper to dry thoroughly between applications. An effective way of using watercolour is to choose one colour, perhaps a blue or sepia, and apply a thin wash of paint and water over the entire surface of the print. When this is dry, you can then paint over the shaded areas using one or two stronger applications of the same colour, carefully blending it in with the brush and kitchen paper or a tissue. Finally, mix in a little

black with the colour to paint in the very darkest tones present in the print. This is known as monochrome painting.

SEALING THE PAPER

After you have selected and tinted your paper, you now must seal the surface before cutting it out. For this you need a shellac sanding sealer or white french polish, sometimes sold as button polish. Using a piece of paper towel, apply the shellac gently over the area to be cut. The shellac will make the paper look a little transparent at first, but after a few minutes this will disappear and, when the paper is dry, you can start to cut. You must seal the surface of all paper used for découpage, not just tinted or coloured photocopies.

CHOOSING A COLOUR

Deciding on the base colour of the object being worked on is an exciting step, which you can approach in two ways. First, decide on a colour that matches an established colour scheme and then choose a design to

complement it, or, second, choose a motif and then select the background colour that enhances it.

If you are thinking of producing découpage commercially, then you will need to use your judgement as to which colours are generally most popular and fashionable. With the projects in this book, it was the designs that came first, and the choice of background colours stemmed from them.

As you will see, the projects illustrated use an enormous range of colours, all of which are water-based emulsion paints. A particular favourite is a rather chalky type of paint that uses natural pigments, and it has a wonderful softness of colour. In the projects where this paint has been used, you can see that when it dries it becomes very much lighter in tone. However, after a coat of varnish it returns to almost the colour it is in the pot. Some companies produce small test pots of emulsion and hundreds of colours can be mixed. These are very practical when you only want to paint a small item. Whichever paint you choose, you may need more than one coat, depending on the object's condition.

CUTTING PAPER

A pair of sharp manicure scissors is essential – the better their quality the easier will be your task. Whether you use straight-bladed or curved scissors is a matter of preference. You will also need a sharp craft knife or scalpel for cutting delicate, fiddly areas, and a mat to cut on. A special cutting mat is worth buying if you are planning several projects, otherwise use a piece of thick cardboard.

The cutting for the early projects is very simple, since you need only to cut around the outer edge of a design. To do this, first roughly cut around the shape to remove excess paper and make the piece easier to handle. Then, start to cut just on or inside the edge or line of your motif, avoiding at all costs leaving a white or coloured edge that will spoil the look of your finished work. Move the paper toward the scissors as you cut and keep your hands relaxed.

When working on more complicated projects, such as the wine coaster (see pp. 92-3), start by cutting out the delicate central areas, since this is tricky to do last when all you have is a flimsy cut-out struc-ture to hold on to. This is where you need to use your craft knife: press firmly on the blade or you will tear the paper rather than slice it cleanly. If using scissors to cut out a central area, pierce the paper with the point of one blade and then enlarge the hole using the scissoring action.

If you are using borders on a curved surface, such as the candlesticks project (see pp. 94-5), you will need to make little cuts along the outer or lower edge of the border at intervals so that you can ease the paper into position without it kinking. A large design, like that used on the fire-screen (see pp. 102-3), will need dividing into smaller sections and reassembling later – it is almost impossible to paste a large section of paper without it crinkling and trapping air bubbles underneath.

ARRANGING AND GLUING

If your are using a number of different motifs, cut out more than you think you need to increase your choice of design possibilities. Working on a flat surface, it is very easy to try out different

arrangements and permutations; on vertical or curved surfaces, however, this can be tricky. In this type of situation, temporarily stick your motifs into position using either a proprietary brand of adhesive plasticine-type dough (which can be removed without leaving a trace) or the type of non-contact repositioning glue that allows you to take up your work and restick it elsewhere. Non-contact glue tends to be a little more accurate than the dough and you will not have to remove your work completely before pasting it permanently into position.

Some designs call for the paper motifs to be overlapped. If so, it is best to start at the top of the object and gradually work your way down the surface, using non-contact glue to hold each piece in place until you have a design you are happy with. Next, of course, you have to remove the motifs from the bottom so that you can get to the ones underneath and then start over again gluing them permanently down from the top. To achieve this, you will either have to remember approximately where all the elements were originally positioned or, if you cannot bear to lose a carefully worked-out design, you will have to make an accurate sketch or take an instant picture snapshot to use as reference.

GLUING TECHNIQUES

For sticking the motifs down permanently, use either a PVA glue or a simple paste of the type available from art supply shops and stationers. All of the motifs in this book were stuck down with paste, which is slower drying than PVA adhesive. This gives you a minute or two to change your mind if you are not quite happy with your first choice of position and more time to smooth out any wrinkles and air bubbles.

Using a brush, paint the surface of the object with the paste, rather than pasting the back of the print. This is always more accurate as well as being a lot less messy. Press the paper firmly down and make sure that you work any bubbles of air out toward the edge of the paper. You may find a lino printing roller helpful for this if you have one, but if not, your fingers will do just as well. Work on a small area at a time, pasting and sticking down as you go. If you have used non-contact glue on a vertical surface, lift a section of the design up, apply the paste, and move on to the next section. When you have finished sticking your design down, leave it to dry for about half an hour, and then remove the excess glue from the surface with a damp sponge. If you have used PVA adhesive, however, you must remove the excess glue straight away or it will dry hard.

It is worth keeping an eye on the piece during this time, so that if an edge starts to lift you can press it firmly down again. If your paper is rather thin, no matter how careful you have been, you may find that after a while it starts to wrinkle slightly, but it will usually shrink back when dry. If you do have an air bubble, make a small incision with the point of your knife to let the air escape, fill the slit in with a little glue, and press the edges of the cut firmly down. Now leave your work to dry thoroughly for at least a further two hours before varnishing. During this time, as long as the paper feels dry, you can cheat a little and disguise any white edges or little blemishes you may have left when cutting-out by going over them with a lead or coloured pencil. And if, by way of an accident or impatience, you have snipped the antennae of a butterfly you can reinstate them with a fine-tipped indelible pen.

TIPS

● Always apply glue to the surface of the object being worked on, not to the back of the motif.

● Paste is slightly slower to dry than a PVA adhesive and so gives you a little time to change your mind about the final position of a motif. Try to handle the paper as little as possible, however, once it is wet with paste.

VARNISHING AND FINISHING

The object you have découpaged will now need between 3 and 20 coats of varnish, depending on the quality of work you wish to achieve and the amount of overlapping, if any, of the motifs. In general, between 10 and 12 coats of varnish is sufficient for most objects. With old-style varnishes you could apply perhaps only a single coat in a day, but with modern water-based products you can speed this up and get on 4 to 5 coats in the same time without difficulty. Make sure you choose a satin varnish, not a matt one. The matting agents used will make the varnish appear cloudy after several coats have been applied.

It is important to work somewhere dust-free when varnishing, and make sure to wear clothing that will not shed hairs or fibres, since these too will settle on the varnish and ruin the overall effect. Make sure that your brush is absolutely clean and free from any paint residue. Apply a thin even layer of varnish and then leave it for at least two hours before applying the next. If, as you start to build up the layers, the varnish does not feel quite dry after two hours, leave it until it does. If you want a professional finish, lightly sand back the penultimate coat with fine-grade sandpaper until you have a smooth finish. Don't do this unless you have applied at least 6 coats of varnish, however, otherwise you could easily damage the outer edges of the print. The final coat of varnish can be either satin or matt, depending on the finish you require.

ANTIQUING

If you decide on an antique finish for your découpage, it is best to apply it after the second coat of varnish has completely dried. It is at this stage that you can still see the texture of the brush marks in the paint, and it is these that help to give the surface finish depth. For the items that have been antiqued in this book, the following recipe was used:

1 part white emulsion paint
3 parts raw umber pigment
8 parts water

As an alternative you could try raw umber acrylic paint, diluted with water to the strength required, or dark-brown emulsion paint diluted with water.

Whichever recipe you choose, the technique is the same. Brush on the antiquing liquid and, with a clean cloth or paper towel, start wiping it off after a minute or so, leaving the colour in the cervices and places where dirt would normally collect. If you want a softer look, don't brush the liquid on, but rub a little in with the paper towel instead. If the whole thing looks like a total disaster, don't worry, just wash it off straight away and start again.

CRACKLE VARNISHING

Crackle varnish is applied on top of the final layer of water-based varnish and it produces a finish resembling that of finely crazed porcelain. The technique uses two different varnishes, both available from art supply shops. The first is slow-drying and oil-based, while the second is a quick-drying, water-soluble one. The cracking occurs due to the difference in the drying time between the two. You next have to rub some oil paint over the surface to re-veal the cracks. This technique does need a little practice to get right, however, and so it is a good idea to try it out on some cardboard first.

Brush the oil-based varnish on to the surface as thinly and evenly as possible, making sure to cover the entire area. This varnish can be quite yellow in colour and so it is easy to see where you have applied it. Leave it for between two and four hours, until it feels dry to the touch when you brush your fingers lightly across the surface but is still just tacky. Next, brush on the water-based varnish in the same way. This time it will be much harder to see where you have applied the varnish and it is even more important that you cover every bit of the surface – hold your work up to the light to check that you have not missed any. When this second coat is dry, after about 30 minutes, you should find that the surface has crazed, although sometimes a little encouragement may be needed by way of some gentle heat. The heat from a lamp or radiator works well, as does that from a hair dryer, but be careful not to put it too close to your work or results may look unnatural.

The next step is to squeeze a little raw umber artist's oil colour on to a saucer and dilute it with a small amount of white spirit to make a more workable consistency. Using a brush or paper towel, work the diluted paint over the surface, making sure that it gets into all the cracks and crevices. Then take a clean piece of paper towel and wipe off the excess paint. If you find that you have some dirty or smudgy areas, this indicates that you have missed this bit with the water-based varnish. A little white spirit applied with paper or a cotton bud will remove the marks and if you are really unhappy with the way it looks, remove all the raw umber, wash off the second coat of varnish, and start again with the first coat.

You must now leave your work overnight so that the oil paint can dry. Bear in mind that the last coat of varnish used is water soluble, so take care not to get it wet. Finally, varnish your piece with a coat of oil-based varnish, either satin or matt depending on the finish required, to protect the surface.

WAXING

A coat of wax over the varnish adds a mellowness and a professional finish. Use a natural-coloured wax or an antique-coloured or a staining wax. Coloured waxes may alter the colour of your work considerably, so be warned. A yellowing antique wax can greatly enhance the spectrum of colours from mid-red through to the yellows and greens, but it is not always successful on blues, tending to make them look a little green. A medium-brown or a natural wax is usually most generally suitable, but you will need to experiment since different brands vary considerably.

A wax finish usually works best on top of matt varnish, so bear this in mind when deciding what the final layer of varnish is to be. If you have used crackle varnish, the sealing coat of oil-based varnish should also be matt, but leave it to harden for at least two days before waxing.

Apply the wax with a soft cloth, working it evenly over the surface. Then leave it to dry for at least 30 minutes before buffing it with a clean cloth. To maintain this finish, a quick coating with aerosol furniture polish every couple of months should do the trick.

Accompanying each project in this book you will find a list of materials required to carry out the work described. Some items of equipment, however, are common to nearly all découpage work, and these are separately listed here.

BASIC MATERIALS KIT

Manicure scissors

Craft knife/scalpel knife

Household scissors

Cutting mat or thick cardboard

Clear shellac

Non-contact glue
or adhesive dough

Paste for final positioning
of motifs

Household sponge

Lead pencil

Satin or matt finish,
water-based varnish

Brushes for gluing, painting
and varnishing

Fine-grit sandpaper

Paper towel

Methylated spirits for cleaning
brushes used with shellac

White spirits for cleaning
brushes used with
oil-based paint

GIFTS

1 Start by choosing which design you want to use from the sheet of scraps (or your other source material). To do this, separate the motifs on the sheet and try out several different examples until you have found the one you are most happy with. Always make sure that the scale is appropriate for the size of the hairbrush being worked on.

2 Using a pair of sharp manicure scissors, cut away the excess paper on the scrap and tidy up any edges as necessary. Apply the glue to the head of the brush, place the scrap on top and press it firmly down. Smooth the paper from the centre out toward the edges to ensure you remove any air bubbles that may have become trapped underneath the paper.

3 Select and cut out a smaller motif and glue it on to the handle, again making sure no air is trapped underneath. If you want to add a painted name, now is the right stage, but leave enough time for the paint to dry thoroughly before wiping off the excess glue with a damp sponge. Leave the brush for a further two hours. Now the brush is ready for varnishing. Apply the varnish with a clean brush in thin, even layers, giving it between 3 and 12 coats in total, and leaving at least two hours between coats. You cannot hurry this stage. If you have used more than 6 coats of varnish, lightly sand back the penultimate coat with a fine-grade sandpaper, but you risk damaging the surface of the paper motif if you have used fewer than 6 coats.

MATERIALS

Hairbrush

Sheets of Victorian scraps, or other source material

Basic materials kit (see p. 19)

1

2

3

VICTORIAN STYLE HAIRBRUSH

It is important to achieve a quick result when starting on a new craft, and so this is an easy, not particularly demanding project to start off with.

The scale of the hairbrush being worked on here is small without being too fiddly, and there is no need to paint or prepare it in any way before commencing, so you can start right in on the fun part.

Another factor that greatly simplifies the découpage process is that this piece uses a pretty Victorian scrap, and so very little cutting out is needed. If, however, you find a motif from another source, such as book or magazine, then you will have to cut it out and prepare it as described in the chapter dealing with materials and techniques (*see pp. 10-19*).

On this brush, a small motif has been added at the end of the handle. If the brush is intended as a gift for, say, a child, you could just as easily paint the recipient's name along it instead, and it would then make an ideal, personalized gift for a lucky somebody.

CARDBOARD
LETTER RACK

Letter racks, such as the one used for this project, are easily found in stationers and gift shops, and if you choose one that already has the right background colour or pattern you will not need to paint it. This letter rack is made from heavyweight, rigid cardboard covered in black paper. As well, it has a fine, gold-coloured border. Even without the découpage it would make a fine gift for anybody who has loads of correspondence to sort out and organize, but once the motif is added it becomes far more personal.

Since the intention is to give this letter rack as a gift, try to select a motif that has significance for the recipient. For example, instead of using a leopard motif, you could find a picture of fish to use for a keen angler, or a picture of a horse for a rider, or a car for somebody who like spending their free time tinkering with a car engine. The black and white print, which has been given an aged effect (*see pp. 10-19*), looks particularly striking on a black background.

1

2

3

4

1 Choose a design from a book containing the prints you want to use and take a black and white photocopy of the one you have chosen. The leopard print used for this project had to be reduced in size so that it would fit within the gold-coloured border already printed on the letter rack.

2 Place a tea bag in a saucer with some boiling water and when it has cooled, wipe the surface of the photocopy with the damp tea bag. The photocopy paper will then take on the yellow-ish colour of old parchment. Leave the stained photocopy on any convenient flat surface until it has completely dried out.

3 Next, seal the photocopy by working clear shellac into the surface using a piece of paper towel. Then, when it has dried, carefully cut out your chosen design using a pair of sharp mani-cure scissors, making sure to leave a clean, neat edge. Apply glue to the front of the letter rack and position the print, making sure to work out any air bubbles. Leave it to dry for 30 minutes and remove excess glue with a damp sponge.

4 Leave the letter rack to dry thoroughly for at least two hours before applying between 3 and 12 coats of varnish. You don't need to varnish the whole rack – just the front where you have stuck the design is sufficient. Take care when varnishing to avoid runs or an excessive build-up on the edges or back of the object.

MATERIALS
Letter rack
Photocopy of an animal print, or other source material
Tea bag
Basic materials kit (see p. 19)

1

2

3

4

1 Using a gold-coloured felt-tipped pen and ruler, draw a line around the edge of the binder on both the front and the back covers. The binder shown here has been given a line of double thickness produced by drawing a second line immediately beneath the first so that the two merge.

2 Seal the page of shell prints by working clear shellac into the surface using a piece of paper towel. Then, when it is dry, cut out the individual motifs using a pair of sharp manicure scissors. It is a good idea to cut more motifs than

you think you will need so that you can experiment with different sizes, shapes and combinations to achieve the best possible design. When organizing the motifs, look at the spaces you are leaving in between the shell images themselves, since these, too, form a part of the overall design. You will probably find it easiest to start with the larger motifs and use the smaller one to fill in the gaps.

3 When you are happy with your arrangement, remove one of the shells, apply paste to the space left, then stick your print

down. Continue in this way until you have covered the whole of the front and then, if you wish, you can repeat the process on the back cover of the binder as well. Wait 30 minutes before removing excess paste with a damp sponge.

4 Give the entire binder 3 base coats of varnish, leaving at least two hours between coats. Then continue varnishing all parts of the binder that have been découpaged, building up a total of about 10 coats.

STUDENT'S RING BINDER

A ring binder like the one above would make an ideal and practical gift for somebody you know going to school or college. Young people love to personalize their possessions – folders, binders and so on – to make them stand out from the crowd, and this one is particularly eye-catching. However, most ring binders you see in stores tend to be very brightly coloured, often in shades of reds, yellows and blues. But if you look around you should not have trouble finding a more subdued one, such as the brown ring binder used here, which provided just the right neutral-coloured background for the beautiful découpaged design of shell prints. Alternatively, you can always paint out a garish cover to provide a plain surface on which to work (*see pp. 10-19*).

If you would rather use one of the bright-coloured binders then shell prints might not be appropriate, so try teaming it up with a design taken from, say, a contemporary piece of gift wrapping for a really unusual effect.

MATERIALS
Ring binder
Prints of shells, or other source material
Gold-coloured felt-tipped pen
Ruler
Basic materials kit (*see p. 19*)

1

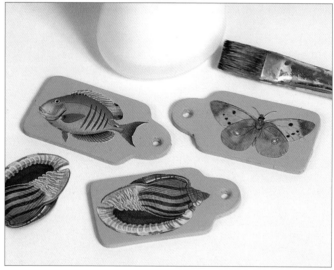

2

1 Start by lightly sanding the key fobs until they feel smooth. If you are making a set, either choose one colour of paint for the background that would be appropriate for all of the cut-outs you are using, or paint the fobs in a variety of colours to enhance the individual print you have chosen for each one. For the fobs illustrated here, light blue was selected for the background to give a feeling of the sea and the sky.

2 Seal your motifs with clear shellac applied with a paper towel, wait for the shellac to dry, and then cut them out using a pair of sharp manicure scissors (*see pp. 10-19*). Coat each painted key fob with paste and carefully arrange your prints on top. Press down firmly with your fingers, taking care to ensure that the edges of the paper are well stuck down. Leave the fobs to dry for 30 minutes and then wipe off the excess paste with a damp sponge. Leave the fobs for a further two hours until they have completely dried. Now you are ready to apply the varnish. Take a clean brush and paint a thin coat of varnish on to the fobs. When this has dried, paint the underside of them with a coat of varnish, and continue in this way, alternately painting the tops and bottoms, until you have as many coats on each side as you require. Key fobs are generally pretty roughly handled so it is a good idea to give both sides at least 8 coats of varnish.

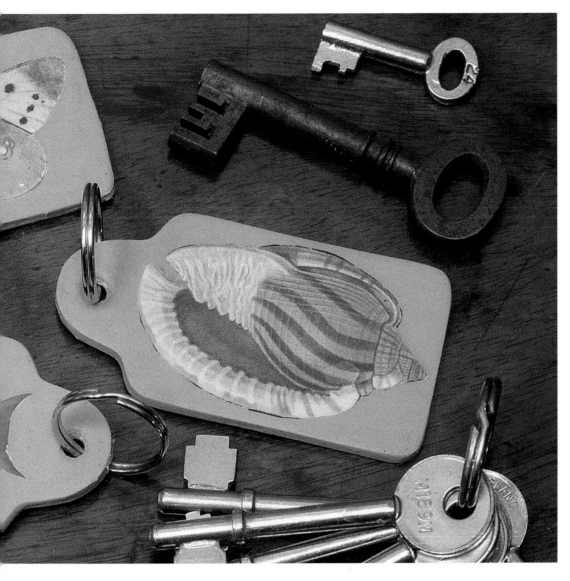

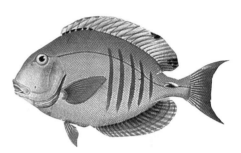

KEY FOBS

With all the keys we seem to accumulate, for the house, car, suitcases and so on, an attractive key fob or two is always welcome. The natural history prints used on these fobs are very appealing and they are just the right size. It is not always easy to find a design appropriate for something so small, so if you do come across a likely motif, put it away somewhere safe until you find the right object.

Other design ideas for use on a key fob include signs of the zodiac, perhaps cut from the horoscope page of a glossy magazine, and the initials of the recipient's in heavy bold type.

The key fobs designed for this project are intended as a set that could be used for the different rooms of a house. You could either paint them all the same colour or give each one a different colour code. They would look fantastic hanging all together in a key cabinet, such as that shown on pages 70-1, or lined up dangling from a simple hook rack. They would certainly make a very simple, inexpensive and practical gift.

MATERIALS
Wooden key fobs
Natural history prints, or other source material
Light-blue paint
Basic materials kit (*see p. 19*)

1

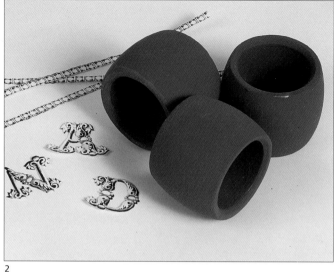

2

3

4

MATERIALS

Plain wooden napkin rings

Red/brown coloured paint

Black and white borders
and initials,
or other source material

Basic materials kit (see p. 19)

1 These initials come from one of the source books printed specifically for découpage work, as do the borders. When you have selected the ones you want, take a photocopy of them, seal the surface with clear shellac applied with paper towel, and leave them to dry before carefully cutting them out (see pp. 10-19). You will need to start the cutting process by piercing the centre of the initial with one blade of the scissors to make a hole you can enlarge to remove the inside, and then cut away all excess paper on the outside to leave a clean edge.

2 Paint the napkin rings in your chosen colour, giving it 2 or 3 coats. It is impossible to paint the whole ring at once, so start by painting the inside and the top edge, and then, when the paint is completely dry, turn it upside down and paint the outside and the remaining edge.

3 Apply paste to the surface of the ring and make sure that you place the initial squarely in the centre. Since you are working on a curved surface, you will need to be a little more persistent than usual in pressing the edges of the paper

down flat. Make sure that no air bubbles are trapped underneath the paper.

4 Glue the borders on to the top and bottom edges of the rings in the same way, easing the edges of the paper to fit round the curved surface. These borders are narrow and the curve was not sufficient to necessitate making the little cuts in the paper described in the materials and techniques section of the book (see pp. 10-19). Finally, remove the excess glue with a damp sponge and apply between 5 and 8 coats of varnish.

INITIALLED NAPKIN RINGS

It is easy to equate the size of the object you are working on with the degree of difficulty involved, but this is not always the case. So don't fall into the trap of imagining that some of the bigger projects in this book represent more of a challenge. In terms of finding a satisfactory arrangement of motifs, larger pieces of découpage can be stretching, but at least you should have an enormous range of papers to chose from that will fit the piece.

These napkin rings are more difficult than the projects you have looked at so far in this chapter because of their curved surfaces, which always makes pasting trickier. Also, the cutting out is more fiddly here and you will need care and patience to remove the initials from the sheet with good, clean edges. See pages 10-19 for more advice on paper-cutting techniques. You may also have to spend a considerable amount of time looking through books and magazines for something that will fit the surface and still look stylish on a dinner table.

ADDRESS BOOK

One of the pleasures of découpage is that you can transform what is really a very ordinary looking object into one that is an attractive and unique work of art. The address book chosen for this project was in desperate need of a new cover to liven it up a little, but it would have been difficult to paint it without also getting at least some of the paint inside on the pages. To overcome this, it was necessary first to cover it with a piece of gift wrap. The piece chosen has very muted shades and no distinctive pattern, and this helped the Victorian scrap design that was used on top to blend in without becoming lost or submerged.

Marbled and tartan papers, and ones decorated with spots or stripes, would also make a suitable background for the découpage, but you will need to choose your motifs very carefully to make sure that there is no clash of colour and design. You could certainly produce some particularly interesting results by choosing a seasonal theme if, for example, you intended the address book to be a Christmas present.

1

2

MATERIALS

Address book

Gift wrap

Victorian scrap,
or other source material

Metal ruler

Basic materials kit (*see p. 19*)

3

1 Select a background paper and a print that work well together. Using manicure scissors, carefully cut away the excess paper from the scrap, tidy up the edges and then put it to one side.

2 Using the book as a template and a metal ruler and craft knife, cut out a piece of gift wrap, allowing about ½in (1.5cm) extra all around and enough to cover the spine. Cut a diagonal piece off each corner so that when you fold the overlap inside the cover, the edges are neatly mitred.

3 Apply the paste to the front cover, place the gift wrap carefully in position on top, make any adjustments, and press firmly down. Working from the centre, apply pressure to make sure you remove any air bubbles. Continue in this way, covering the spine and the back cover. When the cover is dry, paste your motif in place. Wait 30 minutes and then wipe off excess paste. Wait about two hours and then apply 3 base coats of varnish to the whole cover and spine. Continue varnishing the front, which has the motif, until you have as many coats as you require, leaving two hours between each. An address book that will be carried in your bag will need more coats (10 or more) than one that stays at home in a drawer (5 would probably be enough).

1

2

3

4

INTERMEDIATE LEVEL

PENCIL HOLDER

Many people love those old Victorian circus prints, and they look like great fun used here to decorate the pencil holder that is the subject of this project. Once filled with coloured pencils, crayons or pens, it would make a wonderful gift for a child.

Many seemingly throw-away items can be used for découpage and the container here is, in fact, the bottom half of a tall box that originally contained crystallized ginger. It is a good example of the transformation you can bring about with just a little imagination and patience. If you don't have a suitable container, buy any inexpensive one to decorate in this bright and cheerful fashion. Then all you have to do is wait for the smile on your child's face when the gift is opened.

MATERIALS
Pencil holder
Sheets of Victorian circus scraps, or other source material
Bright green paint
Basic materials kit (see p. 19)

1 Paint the outside of the pencil holder a bright shade of green to pick out and emphasize the colours in the clowns' clothes on the scraps. You will need to give it 2 coats to provide a good surface on which to work. When dry, turn the container upside down to paint its base.

2 Using a pair of sharp manicure scissors, carefully cut away the excess paper from the sheets of scraps, leaving a neat, clean edge. You will have more than you need from one sheet of scraps, so spray the back of the individual figures with a non-contact adhesive and experiment with different arrangements of figures until you find the one you like best.

3 Carefully remove the first scrap, apply some paste to the space left on the side of the container, and then reposition the motif and press it firmly down, making sure that the edges are well stuck and that no air bubbles are trapped beneath. Continue in this way until all the scraps are stuck down in position. Wait 30 minutes and remove excess paste with a damp sponge.

4 When the paste is thoroughly dry, apply at least 10 coats of varnish to give the pencil holder the durability needed to withstand plenty of not-too-careful handling by a child, finishing with a satin coat. This will also give the pencil holder just the right level of gloss to enhance the brightness of the base colour and surface motifs.

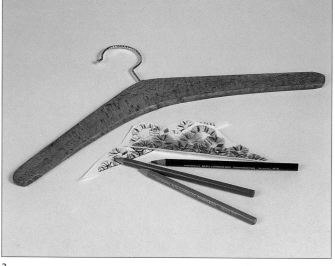

1

2

3

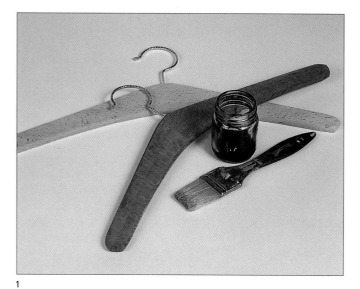

4

MATERIALS

2 coat hangers

photocopies of ribbon
and bow designs,
or other source material

Coloured pencils

Dark shellac

Basic materials kit (see p. 19)

1 Start by lightly sanding the hangers until they feel smooth, making sure to remove all traces of any varnish that may be there, and then stain them with a dark shellac. You can mix in a little clear shellac if you wish to give a lighter tone (as was done with one of the hangers opposite).

2 Take black and white photo-copies of the ribbon and bow design from a source book for découpage and choose two different coloured pencils – here, dark shades of red and blue were used. Using a series of light strokes

next to each, and following the direction of the lines on the print, gradually build up the colour, finishing with the deepest colour in the areas of the darkest shad-ing. Then use a beige-coloured pencil to blend it all together by colouring across the paper from left to right.

3 Seal the paper with clear shellac applied with a piece of paper towel. Pierce the centre of the loops in the bow with one blade of the scissors and cut the middles out first. Once you have finished cutting them all out,

divide each ribbon and bow into three sections and reassemble them so that the design fits the curve of the hanger. The easiest way to do this is to overlap the pieces a little where they join. Paste the design in place in the usual way (see pp. 10-19).

4 When the design is thoroughly dry, apply 3 base coats of varnish to both sides of the hanger, and then continue on the front only until you have as many coats of varnish as you require, but use at least 7. Finish with a coat of matt varnish.

COAT HANGERS

Look in any wardrobe or closet you have at home and you are almost certain to find a plentiful supply of those awful metal coat hangers. No matter how many you throw away, next time you look, there they are back again! Where do they come from?

How nice it would be instead then to receive some attractive, individually découpaged wooden hangers like the ones illustrated here. No need anymore to hide your hangers away inside the wardrobe. Instead you could make a feature of them. Screw a hook to the inside of your bedroom door and hang your nightdress or bathrobe there for all to see. These hangers would also make a lovely gift for a child, decorated with appropriate motifs, such as cartoon characters or animals.

Alternatively, with a little adult supervision and assistance from the father of the household, a decorated hanger or two would make a wonderful Mother's Day present from a child. Looking through magazines and books for ideas, keeping it a secret from Mum, could be all part of the fun.

1 Lightly sand the chest smooth and paint it with dark shellac to stain and seal the wood. Leave it to dry thoroughly.

2 Dilute the ultramarine paint with 4 parts water and paint the chest all over. When you have finished, start with the part you first painted and use paper towel to wipe away some of the paint to reveal the wood beneath.

3 Take photocopies of the borders and swags and colour them with watercolour paints (*see pp. 10-19*).

4 When the paint is dry, seal the watercolour with shellac applied with a paper towel and then carefully cut out the designs with sharp manicure scissors. Paste the bows and swags to the drawer fronts, checking that the motifs on each are all correctly aligned.

5 Glue the borders on to the top of the chest, carefully trimming off any overlap. Wait about 30 minutes and wipe off the excess glue with a damp sponge.

6 Give the entire chest 3 base coats of varnish. Continue to varnish the drawer fronts and top, building up at least 10 coats, and finish with a coat of matt varnish.

1

2

3

4

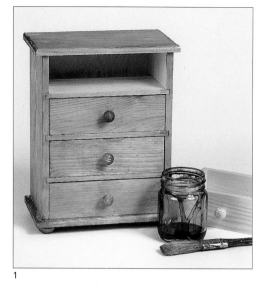

5

6

MINI CHEST

This project is the first in the book in the advanced category, and before tackling it you should have first gained some confidence and experience by undertaking some the easier ones in the chapter. The result is very attractive, but it will take many hours of careful, patient work to achieve it. Once finished, however, it makes a superb gift that would be appreciated by either an adult or a child.

If, after all your hard work, you simply cannot bear to part with it, why not decide to make it as a present for yourself? It would look perfectly at home on your dressing table, as a container for jewellery and little mementoes. A man, however, may prefer a different style of motif, and then it could be used for cuff links, tie pins and similar articles of men's jewellery.

To allow the natural beauty of the wood to show through, a simple colour-wash technique has been used. This is enough to provide background colour without covering the grain, and the little borders and swags have been hand painted with watercolours.

MATERIALS

Wooden mini chest

Photocopies of borders and swags, or other source material

Watercolour paints and brushes

Dark shellac

Light ultramarine paint

Jam jar for mixing

Basic materials kit (*see p. 19*)

CONTAINERS

1

2

3

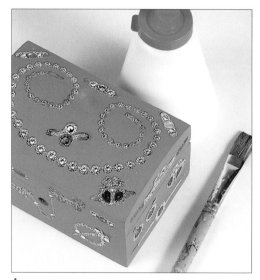

4

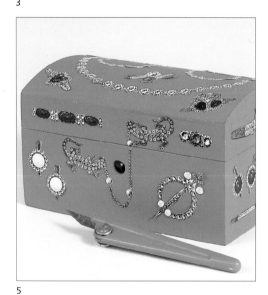

5

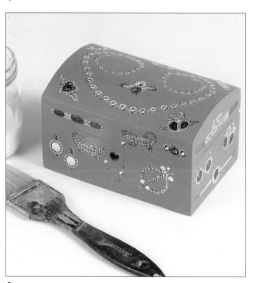

6

1 Start by cutting out more jewellery motifs than you think you need so that you can try out different arrangements. Use sharp manicure scissors and leave a clean, neat edge.

2 Paint the top half of the chest first, wait until it is dry, and then turn it upside down and paint the bottom half. You will need at least 2 coats of paint.

3 Spray the backs of the motifs with a non-contact adhesive and experiment with different design arrangements until you find the one you are most happy with.

4 Remove one cut-out at a time, apply paste to the cabinet, and stick it firmly back in place. Make sure the edges are well stuck and that there are no air bubbles trapped beneath. Continue in this way until you have stuck all the pieces on the front and sides of the chest. Leave the paste to dry for 30 minutes before wiping away excess paste.

5 The lid is a close fitting one so it was possible to stick the lizard and chain brooch over both halves of the box and then split it in two with a scalpel knife when the paste was dry.

6 Give the chest at least 10 coats of varnish to emphasize its jewel-like quality. Leave at least two hours between coats, and sand back the penultimate coat if you want a particularly smooth finish. The top coat of varnish has a satin finish.

JEWEL CHEST

The prints that have been used on this jewel chest were all taken from various catalogues of Victorian-style jewellery. They were already coloured, although rather crudely, but if you want to keep your source material intact, either take black and white photocopies and tint them yourself (*see pp. 10-19*), or take colour photocopies and use them as they are. You will often find pictures like these in glossy magazines.

If you look at the photograph of the finished piece above you will see that although the styles of the motifs are 19th century, the way they have been used, in combination with the wonderful jewel-bright turquoise colour of the paint, makes the chest seem quite contemporary in appearance.

As an alternative design approach, you could cover the chest with black paint to give a dark ground against which to set your découpage cut-outs. This effect would be very different, yet equally striking, and it might then be possible to blend the chest in with an existing colour scheme a little more easily. The decision is yours.

MATERIALS
Wooden chest

Bright turquoise paint

Jewellery motifs,
or other source material

Basic materials kit (*see p. 19*)

SHAKER BOX

These traditional Shaker-style boxes are lovely to decorate. They come in a large range of sizes, which makes them extremely useful for storing all manner of things around the home, and they make especially good sewing boxes.

They look particularly good when painted with natural-pigment colours, which would have been the only ones available to the 18th-century Shakers themselves. Once the paint has dried,

you can decide on the arrangement of motifs you wish to add. Butterflies have been used on the one illustrated here, but Shaker boxes look equally good when decorated with pictures of shells, birds, fish and flowers.

An ageing technique has been introduced on this project, and the colour will blend well with most traditional or contemporary interiors. You can often find pictures of butterflies on gift wrapping paper and in books. If you don't want to destroy your book, simply photocopy the relevant parts. If you find black and white motifs to copy, colour or tint them in your preferred colour scheme (*see pp. 10-19*).

1

2

3

4

1 Lightly sand the whole box with a fine-grade sandpaper and seal the inside by painting it with either a clear or a brown-coloured shellac. Paint the outside with 2 or 3 coats of a dark cream paint. The number of coats you need to use depends on how well the paint covers.

2 Using a pair of sharp manicure scissors, cut out a number of butterflies of different sizes, leaving a neat, clean edge. Don't worry if you accidentally cut off an antenna or two, you can always draw them in again later. Try out different arrangements on the lid of the box. You might find it easier to position the largest butterflies first, and use the smaller ones to fill in the gaps.

3 When you are happy with the design, brush the paste on to the lid of the box and stick each butterfly firmly down. After about 30 minutes, wipe of the excess paste with a damp sponge and leave the box for a further two hours to dry. During this time, if you have accidentally cut off an antenna, draw it back in again with an indelible pen.

4 Apply 2 coats of varnish to both the lid and the base of the box and when it is completely dry, paint on a coat of the antiquing paint (*see pp. 10-19*). As soon as you have painted both parts of the box, start to wipe the paint off with a paper towel and leave it to dry. Continue applying several more coats of varnish, finishing off with a matt varnish. Wait a few days until it is completely dry and apply an antique wax to give a deep, mellow sheen.

MATERIALS
Shaker box
Dark cream paint
Dark shellac
Butterfly motifs, or other source material
Antiquing paint
Antique wax
Basic materials kit (*see p. 19*)

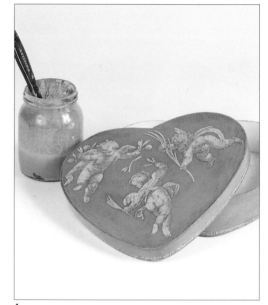

1 Make sure that you fill any little gaps and holes in the box with wood filler and then lightly sand it smooth. Seal the inside of the box with dark shellac and paint the outside of the box with 2 coats of a dusty pink paint.

2 Take your photocopy prints of borders and cherubs and stain them with a tea bag (*see pp. 10-19*). Leave them to dry and then seal them with shellac applied with a paper towel. Wait until they are dry and then carefully cut the motifs out using sharp manicure scissors. Arrange the cherubs on the lid. You need to keep both the unusual shape of the box and the shapes of the motifs in mind in order to achieve a balanced design.

3 Lift each cherub in turn, apply paste to the lid and stick it firmly down. Then follow the same procedure for the borders at the base of the lid and the bottom half of the box. Cut off any excess border material to prevent an overlap where the strip meets itself. Wait 30 minutes and remove excess glue with a damp sponge.

4 Apply 2 coats of varnish to the outside of both halves of the box and then paint on the antiquing paint (*see pp. 10-19*). Wipe away the excess immediately, wait for it to dry completely and continue varnishing until you have as many coats as you require. In order to avoid any problem with the lid not fitting, don't apply more than 3 coats of varnish where the lid overlaps the base.

HEART-SHAPED BOX

These romantic cupids are a particularly appropriate image for a heart-shaped box, and the choice of colour reinforces this theme. The black and white photocopies of the cherubs and borders have been stained with tea and an antiquing paint has been applied to give it an aged appearance (*see pp. 10-19 for details*). The narrow borders add an elegant touch to the sides of the box, but you have to be careful when working on the bottom of a box. If you use too many coats of varnish, you may find that the extra thickness prevents the lid closing properly!

What better present could you give to somebody special in your life on Valentine's Day, especially if you first fill it with delicious chocolates.

MATERIALS
Wooden heart-shaped box
Dusty pink paint
Photocopies of borders and cherubs, or other source material
Tea bag
Dark shellac
Wood filler
Antiquing paint
Basic materials kit (*see p. 19*)

1

2

3

4

MATERIALS
Hinged tin
Cream-coloured paint
Oil-based metal primer
Pansy and shell motifs from gift wrapping, or other source material
Antiquing paint
Basic materials kit (see p. 19)

1 Prime the outside of the tin with an oil-based metal primer and leave it to dry overnight. Apply 2 or 3 coats of a cream-coloured paint and open and close the tin before applying each coat to make sure the hinges are freely working.

2 Using a pair of sharp manicure scissors, cut out the pansy and shell motifs, making sure to leave a clean, neat edge, and arrange a border of pansies around the lid of the tin. Then fill in the middle with a collection of small shells, randomly arranged. When you are happy with the design, take each

motif off in turn, apply paste to the tin and press the paper down firmly, making sure that the edges are well stuck and that no air bubbles are trapped beneath.

3 Using a non-contact adhesive, position more motifs around the base of the tin. Start by centring the pansy design at the front of the tin, leaving enough space for the shell to go beneath. Continue to place the design motifs around each side of the tin until they meet at the back. You may need an extra flower or two to fill a gap or disguise a join. Arrange

the shells below the pansies in a similar way and then use paste applied to the tin to fix them permanently in place. After about 30 minutes, remove excess paste with a damp sponge.

4 With a clean brush, apply 2 coats of varnish to the tin and then rub in the antiquing paint (see pp. 10-18). Keep it fairly light so that you can clearly see the delicate colours of the design. If your motifs overlap, you will need another 10 to 12 coats of varnish, sanding back the penultimate one for a smooth finish.

INTERMEDIATE LEVEL

SMALL HINGED TIN

This unusual and very attractive mix of pansies and shells came from a sheet of gift wrapping paper with a cream background. Sources of design material for découpage are abundant if you keep a sharp eye out for them.

The hinged tin used as the subject of this project has been painted the same cream background colour as that of the paper, but consider a pale shade of pink or purple if you are looking for a brighter alternative scheme. This tin was brand new and so was left plain inside, but if the one you are working on is old and tarnished you could paint the inside, too. Before painting, however, treat any areas of rust (*see pp. 10-19*) or the paint will soon lift.

When painting and varnishing the outside, take particular care in the areas around the hinges. If they become clogged the tin will be awkward to use. When finished, a tin such as this would be ideal for a collection of small shells or if you wanted to fill it with sweets you might consider changing the decorative motif.

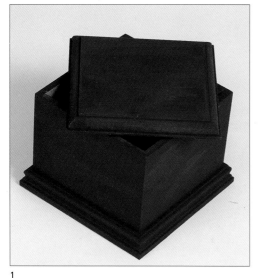

1

3

5

2

4

6

1 Paint the outside of the lid and base of the box with a water-based black paint and, when it is dry, apply another coat.

2 On top of the dry second coat of black paint, apply a coat of red lacquer paint, wait for it to dry and give it another coat of red. When this coat has dried, take some very fine-grade wire wool, dip it in methylated spirits and gently rub the surface of the box in random patches, using a circular motion, to reveal the black paint beneath. To give it an authentic appearance of age, rub the red away in places where you would expect to see normal wear – such as the edges – and pay particular attention to the areas where you don't intend to add any motifs.

3 Using a cotton bud (or your finger), rub gilt cream on to the moulded sections of the lid and base of the box. Leave this overnight to harden.

4 Using a pair of sharp mani-cure scissors, cut out your chosen design. Apply paste to the lid of the box and firmly stick the motif down in the centre. Wait 30 minutes and wipe off the excess paste with a damp sponge.

5 Turn the base of the box on to its side and, following the same procedure in step 4, paste down the borders.

6 Let the paste dry completely for about two hours and then apply at least 12 coats of varnish to the box (*see pp. 10-19*) – more if you want to emphasize its lacquer effect – rubbing back the penultimate coat and finishing with a satin-finish varnish.

ORIENTAL STYLE BOX

This striking oriental-style box has a pattern that was taken from a Chinese china jar that originated in a book of ornamental styles. The découpage technique used here is very simple, but the project has been placed in the intermediate category because of the painted background, which has been especially treated to give the appearance of old, worn lacquer.

The box itself is made out of an artificial composite material known as medium-density fibreboard (which is nearly always referred to simply as MDF), and it is now very commonly used in the cabinet-making industry.

Not only is MDF an inexpensive material, it also has the advantage of being an extremely easy one to glue, drill and screw and, if treated with care, it generally requires no filling or other forms of preparation. Once finished, a box like this would make a very smart spice box or tea caddy, one that would happily grace a display shelf in a kitchen dresser or a dining room sideboard.

MATERIALS
Square MDF box
Black paint
Red lacquer paint
Oriental-style motifs, or other source material
Gilt cream
Cotton bud
Very fine-grade wire wool
Methylated spirits
Basic materials kit (see p. 19)

1

2

3

4

MATERIALS

Oval-shaped wooden box
Green and blue paint
Dark shellac
Prints of fish and shells, or other source material
2 parts of the crackle varnish (*see pp. 10-19*)
Raw umber oil paint
White spirit
Antique wax
Basic materials kit (*see p. 19*)

1 Seal the inside of the box with dark shellac, and put it aside until it is dry. Paint the lid with 2 coats of a mid-green paint and the base of the box with 2 coats of a mid-blue colour of a similar tone.

2 Choose a fish print of the right size for the lid and cut it out carefully using a pair of sharp manicure scissors. When the paint is dry, apply paste to the lid and stick the fish firmly into position, making sure there are no air bubbles trapped beneath. Remove excess glue with a damp sponge after about 30 minutes.

3 Select a number of shell prints in varying shapes and sizes and cut them out. Spray the back with a non-contact adhesive and arrange them around the base of the box. Since this box has no back or front, it is important to position the shell border so that it is even and continuous. An easy way to do this is to choose four of the larger shells of a similar shape (the scallops), and place these at each end and in the middle of both sides. Then arrange more shells in each of the four sections. When you are happy with the design, apply paste to the sides of

the box, stick them in position and remove excess glue with a damp sponge after about 30 minutes.

4 Apply at least 10 coats of varnish. When the last coat is dry, paint on a thin, even coat of oil-based ageing varnish and, when it is still just tacky, brush on a coat of the water-based varnish and leave it to dry (*see pp. 10-19*). Rub raw umber oil paint, diluted with a little white spirit, into the cracks and leave this to dry overnight. Seal the box with 1 coat of matt oil-based varnish and, after couple of days, apply antique wax.

ADVANCED LEVEL

CRACKLE VARNISH BOX

This découpaged box looks great fun to make. Although it has been painted in two different colours, the decorative scheme has been carefully chosen so that both colours give a flavour of the sea, which is very much in keeping with the fish and shell prints that have been pasted on top.

Découpage is a multi-disciplinary craft, and although the design itself is essentially simple, the crackle varnish finish puts it in the category of a more advanced project. If you have not tried to use a crackle varnish finish before, then it is a good idea to practise it first on a scrap piece of wood or on a piece of thick cardboard. If you cannot find coloured prints of fish and shells, you could always photocopy some black and white ones, perhaps from one of the découpage source books that are available in craft shops, and either colour them in yourself or stain them with tea (*see pp. 10-19*). This little box would look charming on a bathroom shelf, perhaps used for storing little tablets of fragrant soap.

1

2

3

4

1 First, seal the surface of the box by applying 1 coat of clear shellac. Wait until it is dry and then brush on 2 coats of blue paint to the outside of the box and the rim of the inside.

2 While the second coat of paint is drying, use a pair of sharp manicure scissors to cut out the roses and cupid motifs, leaving a clean, neat edge. Cut more than you need to give yourself some design flexibility. Nearly all the motifs from a whole sheet of gift wrap were used for the final design on this hat box.

3 Spray the back of the motifs with a non-contact adhesive and arrange them around the base of the box, pasting them permanently into position when you are happy with the arrangement.

4 Arrange the cut-outs on the lid of the box. Start with the central motif and then position the flowers around it so that they relate to the shape of the cherub. You will find it easier to do this if you overlap the roses, cutting off and adding pieces here and there. When you have completed the design, take each off in turn, apply paste to the lid, and stick them firmly in place. Apply 2 coats of varnish to the outside of the box and also to the inside to give it extra strength. When the varnish is dry, brush antiquing paint (see pp. 10-19) on to the outside of the box. Wait for it to dry and then give the box at least 10 coats of varnish, rubbing back the penultimate coat with a fine-grade sandpaper, and finish with a top coat of matt varnish.

HAT BOX

Hat boxes have been in use as ladies' accessories for centuries, and recently they have become extremely popular once again as items to decorate. These boxes lend themselves particularly well to the Victorian style of découpage, with an elaborate, multi-layered design covering their entire surface area.

The hat box used in this project has been given a distinctive Victorian flavour by using individually cut-out motifs from a sheet of gift wrapping paper composed of original scrap designs. As you can see, however, it has a less-cluttered and more-defined design with an overlapping border of roses. This allows the attractive duck-egg blue of the background paint to show through in the spaces.

You can buy new hat boxes in a variety of sizes, and often in stacking sets of three. Older boxes are commonly available in second-hand shops. Once they have been découpaged, they provide a very stylish and practical storage solution for many clothing items other than hats – try using them for scarves, belts and underwear, for example.

MATERIALS
Hat box
Victorian-style wrapping paper, or other source material
Blue paint
Antiquing paint
Basic materials kit (see p. 19)

HOME ACCESSORIES

MATERIALS
Wooden picture frame
Black paint
Victorian scrap borders, or other source material
Basic materials kit (*see p. 19*)

EASY LEVEL

PICTURE FRAME

The Victorian scrap border used to decorate this picture frame was almost a perfect fit just as it was printed, so if you like the appearance of découpage but are not all that keen on the cutting out part, then this could be the perfect project for you to try.

The black-painted background provides a striking contrast to the lilies, but if you find this colour scheme a little too sombre for your taste, why not brighten it up with a green or yellow instead, since both of these colours would make an admiral match for the lily motif. Obviously, you will need to take both the content and coloration of your cut-out motifs into account, and the decor of the room in which the piece will hang when completed, when deciding on paint colour.

The frame used in this example is made of natural wood, and it is a type you will commonly find in department stores. It was brand new and already sealed and so required no special preparation. Although the frame was fitted with clear glass to accommodate a photograph or some other type of picture, you could replace this with mirrored glass and turn it into a stylish mirror suitable for a cloakroom or any other room in your home.

1

2

3

1 Give the frame at least 2 coats of black water-based paint, depending on how well the paint covers. Start by painting the front and then move on to the inside and outside edges, holding the frame by the support at the back.

2 Using a pair of sharp manicure scissors, cut away the excess paper from the scrap border to leave a clean, neat edge and place the border in position on the frame. You will need to trim the ends so that they fit flush at the corners. Brush the paste on to the frame and then stick the paper firmly down, smoothing out any air bubbles from the centre out toward the edges. Leave it to dry for 30 minutes and then wipe off any excess paste with a damp sponge. Leave it for a further two hours to dry completely.

3 Using a clean brush, paint on between 3 and 12 coats of varnish, depending on the finish required. If you have more than 6 coats, sand back the penultimate coat with a fine-grade sandpaper for a really smooth finish, and use satin varnish for the final coat.

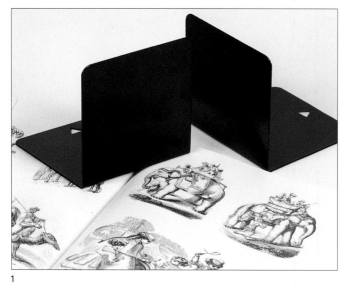

1

2

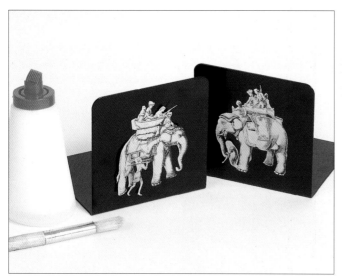

3

4

MATERIALS

Pair of bookends

Black and white photocopies
of elephant prints,
or other source material

Tea bag

Basic materials kit (*see p. 19*)

1 Take a photocopy of a pair of elephant prints and roughly cut them out from their sheet of paper. If you have bought ready painted bookends, such as the ones used here, they will need no special preparation.

2 Place a tea bag in a saucer and add a little boiling water. When it has cooled, rub the damp tea bag over the elephant prints (*see pp. 10-19*), leave the prints to dry and then seal them with a coat of shellac applied with a piece of paper towel. When they are completely dry, use a pair of sharp manicure scissors to cut the elephants out, leaving a clean, neat edge. Start with the more fiddly internal areas first.

3 Brush the bookends with paste and stick the prints into position, carefully smoothing out any air bubbles from the centre out toward the edges. After about 30 minutes, wipe off excess paste with a damp sponge. This is particularly important if your bookends have a dark background colour. Leave the bookends for at least a further two hours to allow the paste to dry properly.

4 Apply between 3 and 12 coats of varnish, leaving at least two hours between coats. Sand back the penultimate coat if you have used more than 6, and finish with either a satin or matt varnish, according to taste.

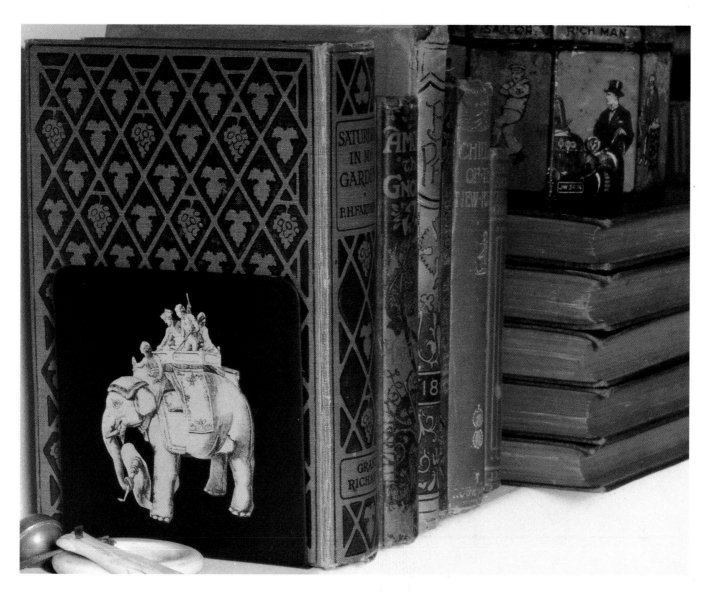

EASY LEVEL

BOOKENDS

The metal bookends used in this project were bought new, already painted black. Similar examples are available in a wide range of colours and slight variations in style, and you could easily buy a pair in a stationery supply shop, department store, and so on.

You don't need to find bookends made of metal, however, since wooden or rigid plastic ones would be just as suitable for this découpage technique.

At some stage, we have all seen bookends made from carved or moulded figures of elephants, usually shown with their heads back and trunks snaking above their heads. It was this type of theme that triggered the idea for the cut-outs used in the bookends pictured above.

Like so many of the motifs used throughout this book, these elephant cut-outs came from a source book printed especially for découpage workers. If you don't want to cut up the book itself, take photocopies of your chosen motifs. The copies used here were stained with tea to give them an aged and interesting appearance.

61

1

2

3

4

1 Choose a flowerpot that has a smooth finish, but if it has the odd lump or bump sand it flush using medium-grade paper. Give the outside a coat of water-based varnish, otherwise your paint will be sucked into the terracotta.

2 When the varnish is dry, give the outside of the pot 2 coats of blue-gray paint. While the paint is drying, seal the card you intend to use with shellac. You may next

have to thin the card to remove some of the paper's bulk. Place your thumb nail between the layers of backing paper and carefully peel off the print (*see pp. 10-19*). Next, use a pair or sharp manicure scissors to cut out your design, starting with the fiddly internal areas first.

3 Apply paste to the outside of the flowerpot and stick your print in place. Use your fingers to

smooth it from the centre out toward the edges to remove any air bubbles trapped underneath. After 30 minutes wipe away excess paste with a damp sponge.

4 When the cut-out is thoroughly dry, apply 10 or 12 coats of varnish, leaving at least two hours between coats. Sand back the penultimate coat with fine-grade sandpaper, and use a satin varnish for the final coat.

MATERIALS
Flowerpot
Postcard of flower print, or other source material
Blue-gray paint
Medium-grade sandpaper
Basic materials kit (*see p. 19*)

FLOWERPOT

You can transform a flowerpot, much like the one used above, into a stunning container for either an artificial or a dried flower arrangement. Don't, however, fill the pot with soil to grow a living plant, since the water would seep through the porous terracotta and eventually lift the decorative finish.

The pot used here was new but if you want to use one from the garden, make sure you clean it thoroughly first.

The motifs used came from book of postcards, but it would not be difficult to find similar prints in book shops and galleries. You can heighten the decorative effect if you découpage two or three pots, place them in a row on a shelf, fill them with moss-covered foam and add an artificial flower to each. Larger pots would allow you to try more elaborate floral arrangements.

1

2

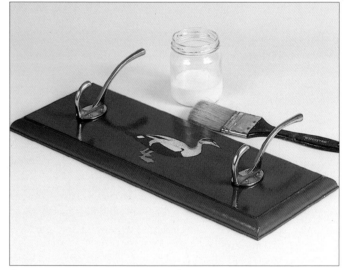

3

4

MATERIALS
MDF hat and coat rack
Colour print of a duck, or other source material
Dark green paint
Medium brown paint
Antique staining wax
Basic materials kit (*see p. 19*)

1 This rack is made from medium-density fibreboard (MDF) and therefore needs no special preparation. Before painting, remove the brass hooks, and then apply 2 coats of dark green paint, making sure you cover all of its surface.

2 When the base green colour is dry, give the moulded edge of the rack 2 coats of medium brown paint, using a small brush for a neat finish. This is not as difficult as it seems, since the moulded edge has slightly less depth than the surface of the rack.

3 While the paint is drying, seal the surface of your colour print with shellac, applied with paper towel (*see pp. 10-19*). Wait for the shellac to dry thoroughly and then, using a pair of sharp manicure scissors, start to cut out the duck motif. Start with the fiddly area between the duck's legs and then move on to the outside of the print, making sure to leave a neat, clean edge. Brush paste on to the centre of the rack and stick the motif firmly in place, smoothing out any bubbles of air trapped beneath from the centre toward the edges. Leave it to dry for about 30 minutes and then remove any excess paste with a damp sponge.

4 After two hours you can start to varnish. Apply 10 to 12 coats, leaving at least two hours between coats. Sand back the penultimate coat and finish with a matt varnish. Leave the rack to dry thoroughly, preferably overnight, and then give it a good coat of antique wax. Wait about 30 minutes and then buff it with a soft cloth for a deep, rich shine. Finally, carefully screw the brass hooks back in place.

EASY LEVEL

HAT AND COAT RACK

This is not only a very simple project to make, at the end of the day you will have an extremely attractive and practical hat and coat rack for the hallway or cloakroom of your home. Or it would look equally stylish if screwed to the back of your kitchen door.

The colours of both the background paint and the printed motifs give this hat and coat rack a decidedly country flavour. If this colour scheme does not suit the position you want to use it in, however, then feel free to choose other colours. Why not, for example, think about a light blue colour to suggest a watery background for the duck motif? You could then rub some gilt cream on to the border if you want to give it an extra decorative touch, choosing a shade that matches the colour of the brass. The choice is yours.

The hat and coat rack used in this project has been finished with an antique staining wax. This is available at hardware and do-it-yourself stores and it adds an important feeling of age and gives a wonderful depth of colour.

1 Wash the jug out with detergent and water and leave it to dry thoroughly. Paint the outside only of the jug with a galvanized metal primer. This will turn the metal black. When the primer has dried, rinse it thoroughly in clean water and let it drain until dry.

2 Paint the exterior of the jug with your chosen colour of paint – here a shocking pink. You will normally need 3 coats of paint to cover when you are using a colour such as this.

3 While the paint is drying, use a pair of sharp manicure scissors to cut out the roses from the sheet of scraps. Spray the back of them with a non-contact adhesive. Begin arranging the motifs around the jug, trying for a design that is balanced but not in any way rigidly symmetrical. Remember that the spaces between your motifs are part of the design, too. When you are happy with the arrangement, remove one motif at a time, apply paste to the jug and stick it firmly back in place. Leave the jug for about 30 minutes and then remove any excess paste with a damp sponge..

4 Wait at least two hours before varnishing. For the jug to look its best, apply at least 12 coats of varnish. Rub the penultimate coat back with a fine-grade paper and give a final coat of satin varnish.

1

2

GYPSY STYLE JUG

This bright and cheerful jug has a wonderful fresh gypsy-like quality to it, and it is not dissimilar to the decorative approach of certain types of barge ware.

The galvanized jug itself was bought new from a hardware store, and because it was decided to leave it unpainted on the inside, it could still be used as a container for fresh-cut flowers. A large bunch of roses in an array of different colours, picked fresh from the garden, would set off the découpage decoration to perfection.

If the deep shocking pink that has been chosen for the background colour on the outside of the jug is a little bright for your taste, you could always substitute a deep shade of blue, for example – even a green-blue colour would be suitable as a background for the surface decoration.

The flowers used here came from a sheet of scraps and so required very little in the way of cutting out. If you are using other source material, always cut out the fiddly internal areas first and then move on to the outside parts.

3

4

MATERIALS

Galvanized jug

Galvanized metal primer

Shocking pink paint

Sheet of rose scraps,
or other source material

Basic materials kit (*see p. 19*)

1 Sand back the wood if necessary and then brush a dark shellac over the sconce to take away its new colour and give it more of an aged appearance.

2 Paint the sconce with just 1 coat of paint. When it has dried, sand it back with a medium-grade paper to reveal the grain of the wood beneath. Remove more of the paint in those areas where the sconce would naturally receive wear and tear when in use.

3 Photocopy a cherub print, or your own source material, and stain it with a damp tea bag (*see pp. 10-19*). Seal the print with clear shellac applied with a paper towel and, when it is dry, use sharp manicure scissors to cut the motif carefully out, starting with the delicate internal areas. You may find this easier with a scalpel knife rather than scissors.

4 Brush paste on to the sconce and stick your motif down. Apply pressure from the centre of the paper out to the edges to remove any air bubbles that may be trapped beneath. Wait about 30 minutes and remove excess paste with a damp sponge. Apply 10 or 12 coats of varnish. Rub the penultimate coat back with a fine-grade paper and give a final coat of matt varnish.

1

2

3

4

WALL SCONCE

The very delicate cherub design selected for this wall sconce looks best on a soft, muted background colour, and the extremely attractive shade of blue paint that has been used here comes from an exclusive range of traditionally made historic colours.

The first stage in the preparation of the sconce involved sanding back the wood to reveal and accentuate the grain beneath. Both the wood and the print have been given an ageing treatment (*see pp. 10-19*) and this, as well as the patience and skill required for cutting out the motif, make it a more difficult project than some others you have seen so far in this chapter.

Your patience will be more than amply rewarded, however, when you finally hang this elegant sconce on the wall of your dining or sitting room and light your first candle.

1 Lightly sand the cabinet until it is smooth, and then give the central panel 2 coats of a dark cream paint and wait for it to dry.

2 Place strips of masking tape down the edges of the central panel to protect it and then paint the surround and the rest of the cabinet with the dark blue-green paint. This may need a second coat, depending on how well the paint covers the wood.

3 While the paint is drying, seal the postcard with shellac and then thin the paper backing by putting your thumb nail between the print and the layers of backing and carefully peeling them apart (*see pp. 10-19*). Using a pair of sharp manicure scissors, cut out the motifs, apply paste to the cabinet and stick the motifs in position, placing the stems right at the bottom edge of the panel. Remove excess glue after 30 minutes using a damp sponge.

4 Give the cabinet 2 coats of varnish all over and then apply the antiquing paint (*see pp. 10-19*). Wipe this off, leaving colour only in the brush marks and crevices. Apply another all-over coat of varnish and then continue on the front panel only with a further 8 to 10 coats. Give the entire cabinet a final coat of matt varnish and, when it is dry, apply an antique wax and buff to a deep, mellow shine.

1

2

3

4

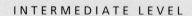

INTERMEDIATE LEVEL

KEY CABINET

This key cabinet has been given a folk art look by painting the central panel cream and then using a stylish tulip print on top. The print came from a book of postcards, and these are a treasure trove of ideas for découpage artists. The dark blue-green coloured paint used on the rest of the cabinet was selected principally because it goes so well with the colour of the leaves of the tulip but, as an alternative, you could consider a shade of red that tones with the colours of the flowers, and this should look just as good.

The cabinet has been given an antique look by using an application of raw umber paint and, as a finishing treatment, it was treated with an antique wax, which has completely transformed its appearance.

This little cabinet not only looks extremely attractive, is also very useful for storing all those different sets of keys we all seem to accumulate. You could, if you wish, co-ordinate the motifs on the cabinet with those of the key fobs, which are the subject of an earlier project (*see pp. 28-9*).

MATERIALS

Wooden key cabinet

Dark cream paint

Dark blue-green paint

Postcard of tulips,
or other source material

Masking tape

Antiquing paint
(*see pp. 10-19*)

Antique staining wax

Basic materials kit (*see p. 19*)

1

2

3

4

MATERIALS

Metal tray
Oil-based metal primer
Cream-coloured water-based paint
Prints of fruit and butterflies, or other source material
Antiquing paint (see pp. 10-19)
Oil-based polyurethane varnish
White spirit for cleaning varnish brush
Basic materials kit (see p. 19)

1 Wash the tray thoroughly in detergent and hot water and make sure that it is clean and free from all traces of grease. Leave it until it is completely dry. Paint the tray all over with 1 coat of an oil-based metal primer to provide a suitable surface for the water-based paint to adhere to.

2 When the primer is dry, paint the tray with 2 or 3 coats of the cream-coloured paint and, while it is drying, begin to cut out your fruit prints using sharp manicure scissors. Arrange them on the tray and then choose a

butterfly, or other appropriately sized insect, to link the space between the two cut-outs.

3 When you are happy with the arrangement, lift each motif in turn, apply paste to the tray and stick the print firmly in to place, smoothing out any air bubbles that may be trapped beneath toward the edges of the paper. Wait for about 30 minutes and then wipe off excess paste with a damp sponge. If you have snipped off the butterfly's antennae, which is easy to do, draw them back in now with an indelible pen.

4 Give both sides of the tray 2 coats of varnish and, when it is dry, apply the antiquing paint to one side of the tray (see pp. 10-19). Straight away, begin to wipe off the excess, leaving colour only in the brush marks and crevices. Allow this side to dry, turn the tray over and antique the other side. When the paint is dry, give both sides another 2 coats of varnish, and continue to varnish the décou-paged side only with another 8 to 10 coats. To make the tray resist-ant to spills and heat, apply 2 coats of oil-based polyurethane varnish in either a satin or a matt finish.

FRUIT TRAY

These lovely prints of fruit and butter-flies provide a very appropriate theme for a tray. As a purely decorative piece, it would look charming standing on a sideboard or coffee table. If, however, you want it to be practical and heat-proof, you will need to apply 2 coats of an oil-based polyurethane varnish on top of the layers of acrylic varnish.

The flexibility you have in design terms of using prints such as these means that you can decide to use vir-tually any background colour. But the cream-coloured paint used on the tray illustrated above looks particularly effective when teamed with the antiqu-ing paint technique (*see pp. 10-19*).

This particular tray was made of gal-vanized steel. It was bought new and was already coated with a lacquer fin-ish. As a first step, it was therefore painted with an oil-based metal primer, rather than a primer designed for galvanized metal. A wooden tray would make a perfectly suitable alter-native, although you would them omit the oil-based primer and use a water-based paint directly on the wood.

1

3

2

4

1 Paint the wastepaper bin on all sides with an oil-based metal primer to provide a base for the emulsion paint to adhere to. Bear in mind that the inside of the bin may take a lot of time to dry.

2 Brush on 2 or 3 coats of white emulsion paint over the primed surfaces. Again, the inside of the bin will take extra time to dry, so allow plenty of time between coats of emulsion.

3 Take a photocopy of a design and appropriate borders from a découpage source book. You will need about 6 to 8 strips of borders to fit around both the top and bottom of the bin. Cut around the outside edge of the print with a pair of sharp manicure scissors and paste it in place in the centre of the bin. Cut both sides of the borders and stick them in position. When pasting, always apply the paste to the surface of the object, not to the back of the motif, and ensure no air bubbles are trapped beneath by applying pressure from the centre out toward the edges.

4 Apply 10 coats of varnish to the outside surface of the bin and 3 to the inside and bottom. Leave about two hours between coats. When the bin is completely dry, apply dark shellac to the surface with a soft cloth, working quickly and using a steady, circular motion. Then leave it to dry. This may look a patchy at first, but after several layers of the shellac have been applied, its appearance will start to even out. Build up 6 or more coats in this way, leaving about 30 minutes between coats.

MATERIALS

Metal wastepaper bin

Oil-based metal primer

White emulsion paint

Photocopies of borders and
design, or other source material

Dark shellac

Soft cloth

Basic materials kit (*see p. 19*)

INTERMEDIATE LEVEL

WASTEPAPER BIN

The print on this wastepaper bin looks impossibly complicated to cut out of a sheet of paper. Well don't worry, you won't have to because there is a very simple way to cheat in order to achieve this effect. When applying a black and white print to a white background you

only need to cut around the outer edge of the motif and, once you have covered it with several layers of varnish, the difference between the natural white background of the paper and the paint becomes imperceptible.

Try using this technique with very intricate prints or where there are a lot of plant fronds in the design. In total, the bin had 10 coats of varnish and then it was given a treatment similar to french polishing, consisting of 6 coats of brown shellac on top of the varnish.

1

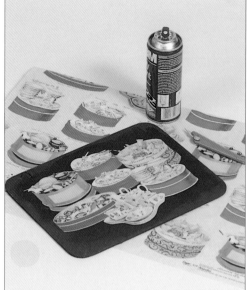

3

4

1 Give each place mat 2 coats of paint – here, one mat was painted green and the other blue.

2 While the paint is drying, cut out your motifs using manicure scissors. Arrange the tea set cut-outs on the blue mat, and try different arrangements – start at the top of the mat and work down. It may help to spray the back of the motifs with a non-contact adhesive to keep them in place.

3 Arrange the cups and saucers on the green mat. If you want to keep your designs accurate, outline the arrangement on both mats using light pencil or chalk marks and make a sketch of the final positions of the cut-outs before removing them. Starting with the top-most motif, paste it firmly into position, and continue in this way working down the piece. Apply paste to the overlapping paper as necessary where

one motif sits on top of another. Check carefully that the prints are firmly stuck down where they overlap. Wait about 30 minutes and then remove excess paste with a damp sponge.

4 The overlapping layers of paper will require at least 10 coats of varnish and then 2 coats of an oil-based polyurethane varnish to make the mats resistant to heat and spills.

MATERIALS

Place mats
Prints of china, or other source material
Dark blue water-based paint
Dark green water-based paint
Oil-based polyurethane varnish
White spirit for cleaning varnish brush
Basic materials kit (*see p. 19*)

PLACE MATS

Place mats would ordinarily make a good choice for a first try at découpage. Their large, flat surfaces lend themselves to almost any decoration. However, the motifs have been arranged in overlapping layers, making this project a little more difficult than those earlier in the chapter. The antique cups and saucers used on the mats above were found in a magazine and those of the toy tea sets came from a sheet of gift wrapping. Together, the designs make a very appropriate theme.

If you want your place mats to be decorative as well as practical, apply 2 top coats of an oil-based polyurethane varnish over between 10 and 12 coats of ordinary water-based varnish. This should be enough to make the mats both heat and spill proof.

1

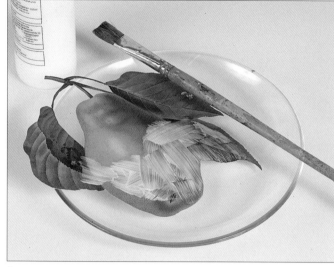

2

3

4

MATERIALS

Glass plate
Print of fruit, or other source material
PVA glue
Light green paint
Basic materials kit (see p. 19)

1 Choose a fruit design that is an appropriate size to fit under your plate. Using a pair of sharp manicure scissors, carefully cut the print out, starting with the delicate internal areas first, leaving a clean, neat edge all around.

2 Apply an even coating of the PVA glue to the surface of the motif, taking particular care that you cover every bit of the print area, and especially the edges.

3 Stick the print firmly to the underside of the plate, squeezing out any air bubbles by applying pressure from the middle of the paper out toward the edges. Because of the curve of the plate, the edges of the paper may tend to lift and you will need to apply pressure with your fingertips until you are confident that the cut-out is securely in place. As soon as it is, remove excess glue from the plate with a damp sponge and leave it to dry for a couple of hours.

4 Before starting to paint your plate, check one final time and make sure that every part of the print is well stuck down. If it is not, the paint will quickly find its way under any area that is loose and ruin all your hard work. When all is well, brush the back of the plate with 2 coats of light-green paint and then apply 2 or 3 coats of varnish to seal the surface and protect the painted surface against knocks and abrasion.

WORKING ON GLASS

You need to employ a slightly different découpage technique when you come to work on transparent glass objects. In this case, you need to apply the adhesive to the front of the paper motif and then stick the print to the underside of, say, a plate or dish, or to the inside of a vase or bowl.

With the glass of the object acting as the surface of your work, you then need only to varnish the back of the print to seal and protect it. Rather than paste, you will have to use a special PVA glue because it is both strong and, most importantly, is completely transparent when dry.

The pear design used here makes a very attractive fruit plate. If you like the effect, why not make a set of plates using different fruits on either the same or differing backgrounds? A plate like this would not be suitable for everyday use, however, and it is certainly not dishwasher proof. Don't leave it to soak in water either – carefully sponge it clean, then dry it and use it for special occasions only.

1

2

3

4

1 Wash the bucket in detergent and hot water to remove all traces of grease, allow it to dry and then paint it inside and out with 1 coat of galvanized metal primer. When it has turned black and is dry, wash it off thoroughly and leave to drain dry.

2 Next, give the bucket, inside and out, 2 coats of the dark green paint. Because the handle touches the rim of the bucket, you will need to apply each coat of paint in two stages, allowing the handle to rest on alternate sides of the bucket while the other dries.

3 Using a pair of sharp manicure scissors, carefully cut out the two flower prints, starting with the delicate internal areas first. You may be happier using a scalpel knife. Apply paste to the surface of the bucket and glue the sunflower print in place. Since this is a large motif, you need to take particular care not to trap air bubbles underneath – so smooth the print down from the centre out toward the edges.

4 Stick the dandelion print on to the other side of the bucket in the same way. Wait 30 minutes

and then remove excess paste with a damp sponge. Wait about two hours for the paste to dry out thoroughly before varnishing. Apply 3 base coats of varnish to all surfaces, inside and out. Give the outside only at least another 8 coats, sanding back the pen-ultimate one for a smooth finish.

BUCKET CONTAINER

The printed motifs used for this project came from a book of wonderful old botanical prints. As well as the attractive subject matter they depict, part of their appeal also lay in the fact that they are perfectly proportioned for the bucket container to which have been applied.

This bucket has been painted a dark green colour, but the design would look equally appealing on a light green or a blue-green ground, and it makes the perfect container for a small tree or some other large plant.

If you want the bucket to be completely practical, do not paint its inside surfaces. If, however, you do decide to paint it, as in this example, you will have to place a saucer or some other container inside to protect the paint finish from water damage. There was little point in giving the bucket an antique treatment, since on such a dark background the effect would hardly be visible, but you could give it a coat of antique wax for a more mellow and aged appearance.

MATERIALS
Galvanized bucket
Galvanized metal primer
Dark green water-based paint
Appropriately sized prints of flowers, or other source material
Antique wax (optional)
Basic materials kit (*see p. 19*)

1

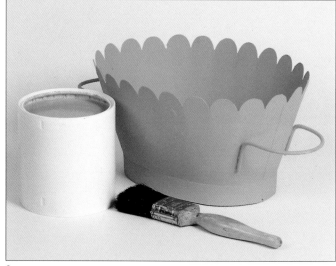

2

3

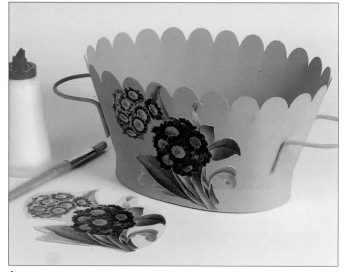

4

MATERIALS
Metal planter
Oil-based metal primer
Yellow paint
Prints of flowers, or other source material
Antiquing paint
Basic materials kit (see p. 19)

1 Wash the planter thoroughly with detergent and warm water to remove all traces of dirt and grease and then leave it to dry. When it is dry, paint it with an oil-based metal primer, both inside and out, and leave it to dry completely, preferably overnight.

2 Apply 2 coats of deep yellow paint over all the primed surfaces, allowing the paint to dry properly between coats.

3 The pansy has a very delicate structure so you will need to take considerable care when

cutting. Use a sharp scalpel knife and start with the delicate internal areas first and then move on to the outside edges. Apply paste to the planter and carefully stick the flower in position, carefully smoothing out any air bubbles that may be trapped beneath. Don't worry if you have snipped a stem in half, since you can join it together again at this stage.

4 Cut out the auricula and paste it on the other side of the planter in the same way and, after about 30 minutes, remove excess paste with a damp sponge. When

the paste has dried, apply 2 base coats of varnish to all the surfaces, leave to dry, and then brush antiquing paint on the outside of the planter (see pp. 10-19). Almost immediately wipe off the excess, leaving the colour in the brush marks and crevices only. Leave it to dry and then repeat this process on the inside and bottom of the container. Apply at least 10 more coats of varnish to the external decorated surfaces of the planter.

DECORATIVE PLANTER

With an object such as this planter to work on the choice of flower motifs is an obvious one, and the pictures of pansies and auriculas provide a striking contrast to the deep-yellow background colour the planter has been painted. An alternative decorative theme could be pictures of insects, especially those friendly to plants such as bees and ladybirds.

If you want to use a less strident background colour, consider a light green or cream-coloured paint, both of which should fit in with most room colour schemes around the home.

Decorated in this fashion, the planter would look ideal either in a conservatory or in a dining room. Its overall shape would accommodate several small pots of flowers, but make sure that you protect the bottom of the planter with small saucers to catch excess water draining from the pots. If you don't need a planter, then it would also make an attractive container for fruit or nuts, and you could choose a different set of motifs.

LAMPSHADE AND BASE

Although both the lampshade and base used in this project were bought separately from different stores, the découpage treatment that has been applied has united them perfectly to produce a handsomely matched pair. Although the leaf and insect motifs that have been used are old, the light colouring of the lamp means that this lampshade and base would fit in well with most modern decorative styles.

The lampshade is made out of paper while the base is made of wood, and so the preparation required before starting work is minimal. However, any time saved at this stage of the operation is certainly lost in the cutting out of the leaves, which have all those serrated edges, and require careful and patient treatment! The insects motifs were selected because of their colouring, which blends so well with the leaves and the base of the lamp.

1

2

3

4

MATERIALS
Wooden lampbase
Paper lampshade
Medium-grade sandpaper
Prints of leaves and insects, or other source material
Basic materials kit (*see p. 19*)

1 Lightly sand the base of the lamp in order to remove some of the shine and to provide a good surface for the paste and varnish to adhere to.

2 Start to cut out the prints of leaves, using a pair of sharp manicure scissors or a scalpel. Start with the delicate internal areas first, taking particular care with the ones that have a fiddly, intricate design. It is best to cut out more leaves than you think you need so that you have some flexibility to experiment with different design arrangements.

3 Spray the back of the leaf motifs with a non-contact adhesive and then try out different design arrangements around the base of the lamp. When you are completely happy with your design, remove the motifs, one at a time, brush the base with paste and stick each one firmly back in position, making sure to remove any air bubbles. Because of the curved surface of the base, the edges of the leaves are likely to spring up, so take particular care in pressing the edges well down. After about 30 minutes, remove excess glue with a damp sponge.

5

6

7

8

4 Apply 10 to 12 coats of varnish to the base, leaving about two hours between coats. Lightly sand back the penultimate coat for a smooth finish, and give a top coat of matt varnish.

5 Brush 1 coat of clear shellac on to the inside of the shade to seal the paper, and apply 1 coat to the outside as well.

6 While the shellac is drying, cut out several insects of differing sizes and varieties. If you can, try to keep the legs and antennae in place, but don't worry too much if you accidentally cut some off, since you can always draw them in later or stick them together again when pasting.

7 Now spray the backs of the insect motifs with a non-contact adhesive and try out different design arrangements until you find one you like. Then remove the motifs, one at a time, brush paste on to the shade and stick the motifs back in position. Take particular care when removing the excess glue, and use a barely damp sponge so as not to damage the paper of the shade.

8 Apply between 10 and 12 coats of varnish to the outside of the shade, very lightly sanding back the penultimate one, and finish with a matt top coat.

ADVANCED LEVEL

WATERING CAN

Watering cans are very common, everyday sorts of objects. They are, however, particularly rewarding objects to découpage because of the near total transformation you can bring about.

Once filled with flowers, fresh cut or dried, this watering can would look at home in the kitchen, for example, or it would also make a valuable decorative contribution in a conservatory or sunroom.

The fruit, flower and vegetable motifs used here were found on different sheets of gift wrapping. They are certainly an appropriate decorative theme, but their colours are a rather unusual mix, however, so take care with your choice of background paint. Dark green would have been a good choice in place of the blue or, for a really vibrant look, you could go for orange.

The motifs are not at all taxing to cut out, apart from the sunflowers, but the overlapping arrangement on a vertical surface makes this project a little tricky. You can leave the inside of the watering can unpainted if you like so that it can still be used as a waterer.

1

2

3

4

1 Wash the watering can thoroughly in detergent and warm water to remove any dirt and grease and leave it to drain dry. When dry, paint the outside of the can with primer and, when it has turned black and has dried, wash it carefully again in clean water.

2 Paint the outside of the watering can with 2 coats of dark blue paint and, while it is drying, cut out between 30 and 40 motifs. The finished watering can here has an arrangement of 30 prints, but the additional ones will give you extra design choices.

3 Spray the backs of half the motifs with a non-contact adhesive and arrange them on one side of the watering can, starting from the top and working down. Some of the cut-outs are rather bright so think about the overall colour balance of your design. When you have found an arrangement you like, start on the other side of the can. You may be able to use the first design as a guide and paste the second set of motifs permanently down straight away. Always apply the paste to the object, not the motifs. The designs can differ slightly from side to side.

Now turn your attention back to the first side, remove the motifs one at a time, and paste them permanently in position. Finally, paste some of the motifs on to the top of the watering can.

4 Apply between 10 and 12 coats of varnish to all the decorated outside surfaces, leaving about two hours between coats, and sand back the penultimate one for a smooth finish.

89

1 Clean the jug in detergent and water and allow it to drain dry. Using a sheet of coarse sandpaper, remove all traces of loose and flaking rust, and then paint the outside with 2 coats of a combined rustproofer and metal primer. Leave the handle until last so that you have something to hold while painting. Leave the jug overnight to dry.

2 Apply 2 or 3 coats of the light green background colour to the primed surface, again leaving the handle until last.

3 Using a craft knife, cut out the prints of roses, starting with the delicate internal areas. The structure of the roses is very fragile and if you do have a break in a stem, you can reunite it at the pasting stage. Spray the back of the prints with a non-contact adhesive and experiment with different arrangements. If you have one or two gaps, cut out some butterflies and use them as fillers. Lift the top section of one of the roses, apply paste to the jug and stick that section back. Continue down like this until the motif is all stuck down and then turn your attention to the next rose. Finally paste the butterflies in place. Wait 30 minutes before wiping off excess paste with a damp sponge.

4 Paint on 2 base coats of varnish and then apply the antiquing paint (*see pp. 10-19*). Immediately remove the excess, leaving colour in the brush marks and crevices only. Wait for it to dry, and continue to build up another 8 to 10 coats of varnish.

1

2

3

4

ADVANCED LEVEL

ENAMEL JUG

Although it doesn't look like it now, the jug opposite was bought for next to nothing in a junk shop. It was rusty and appeared to be beyond repair.

Once découpaged, however, it makes a marvellous decorative item, one suitable for almost any room in the house.

The attractive rose print motifs are difficult to cut out because of the thorns and the serrated leaf edges, but the results make the trouble worthwhile. For subjects like this, you may find a scalpel more convenient than scissors.

The jug has been given a light green background colour, but most shades of green and blue would look good with the roses. The inside of the lip has been painted but not the inside proper, since it is hardly visible through the jug's narrow opening.

MATERIALS

Enamel jug

Coarse-grade sandpaper

Combined rustproofer
and primer

Light green paint

Prints of roses and butterflies,
or other source material

Antiquing paint
(see pp.10-19)

Basic materials kit (see p. 19)

ADVANCED LEVEL

WINE COASTER

This wine coaster would look very elegant on the dinner table, one set either for a formal or an informal dinner party. An appropriate burgundy colour has been selected for the background, although a shade of dark green would be just as good a choice. In this regard, you need to be guided by the colour and style of the crockery it will be seen against, or with the colour and style of the table centrepiece, for example.

The border used on the coaster comes from a border of grapes taken from a source book printed for découpage workers, but you often see very attractive wine labels featuring small bunches of grapes and other wine- and vineyard-orientated motifs, which you could use instead. Rather than cut up the original book, the borders you see above were first photocopied.

For a finishing touch of chic, the coaster was given a gold rim of gilt cream. The shape and size of the coaster make this is a more difficult project than some others, and also the border requires extremely precise cutting out if it is to look really professional.

1

2

3

4

1 Paint the coaster if necessary with an oil-based primer, and after it has dried give the top and the inside of the coaster 2 or 3 coats of the burgundy-coloured paint. When this has dried, paint the bottom of the coaster in the same way.

2 Very carefully cut the photo-copy of the intricate design of the border using sharp manicure scissors or a scalpel knife. Start with all the delicate internal areas first, and then cut the outer edge of the border to leave a clean, neat finish. Taking care not to tear

it, wrap the cut-out around the coaster to determine the length required and trim off any excess. Apply paste to the coaster and stick the border firmly down in position. Use the seam on the coaster as the joining point for the two ends of the border and, after about 30 minutes, wipe away any excess paste with a damp sponge.

3 To apply the gold border to the rim, dip your finger, or a cotton bud, into some gilt cream and apply it to the coaster. Leave it to dry for at least 24 hours before starting to varnish.

4 Apply between 10 and 12 coats of varnish, leaving two hours between coats. Sand back the penultimate coat for a smooth finish and use either satin or matt varnish for the top coat.

1

2

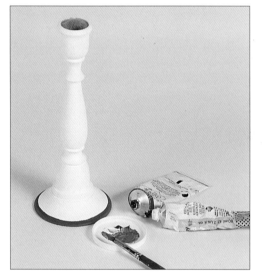

3

4

5

6

1 Choose border prints that are appropriate in both scale and style for your candlesticks and take photocopies of them.

2 Paint the candlesticks with 2 or 3 coats of white emulsion paint, depending on how it covers. Allow the paint to dry.

3 Using a fine brush, paint the base rim of the candlestick with ultramarine acrylic paint to match the borders and give it additional visual weight.

4 Brush a thin wash of ultramarine watercolour paint over the entire surface of the border print and leave it to dry. Using a fine brush, apply a deeper shade of the paint to pick out shadowy areas of the border – use the shading of the print as a guide. Leave it to dry. Finally, add a little black paint to the blue in order to emphasize the very darkest parts of the border. When the paint is dry, seal the print with clear shellac applied with paper towel.

5 Carefully cut out all the borders with sharp manicure scissors or a scalpel knife. Take the borders that are going around the curved surface and make little vertical cuts along the edge at frequent intervals so that the paper can be eased into position. Apply paste to the candlesticks and stick the borders in position. Trim off the excess where the ends meet.

6 Apply between 10 and 12 coats of varnish, waiting two hours between coats, and use fine sandpaper on the penultimate coat for a smooth, professional finish.

MATERIALS

Wooden candlesticks

White emulsion paint

Ultramarine acrylic paint

Ultramarine and black
watercolour paints

Photocopies of borders,
or other source material

Basic materials kit (*see p. 19*)

ADVANCED LEVEL

CANDLESTICKS

The inspiration for these découpaged wooden candlesticks has come from the classic blue and white designs of Delft china, and the decorative treatment would make them eminently suitable for a bedroom or bathroom setting. Borders from a découpage source book have been used here, tinted with three tones of ultramarine watercolour paint.

In order to ease a flat design around the curved surface of the candlesticks, the borders had to be cut at intervals to make them sit properly. You should, of course, use a background colour and decorative theme that ties the candlesticks in with the room setting in which they will be seen and, if you wish, you could also give them a crackle varnish finish (*see pp. 10-19*).

HOUSEHOLD FURNITURE

1 Fill the old screw holes and any other defects in the chair's surface with wood filler. Sand the filler back flush and then sand back all of the wood to achieve a good, smooth finish.

2 Give the chair 2 coats of red paint. Apply the paint in two stages – first the top, then, when it is dry, the underneath parts.

3 Rub the surface of the chair in random areas with a candle, following the grain of the wood. You will need to press fairly firmly to transfer sufficient wax to the chair. Then, using clear wax polish and a cotton bud, add some blobs of wax to the chair, again at random. Leave the wax to dry hard for a few hours.

4 Now paint the chair with 1 coat of blue paint. When it is completely dry, use sandpaper to rub back the surface to reveal random areas of red paint beneath. This will be easiest to do where you have used the wax resist.

5 Cut out the toy motifs with manicure scissors and place them over the seat of the chair. When you have a balanced design, apply paste to the chair and stick the motifs firmly down. Wait 30 minutes and remove excess paste with a damp sponge.

6 Spray the remaining prints with a non-contact adhesive and arrange them on the back of the chair. When you are happy with the design, stick the motifs in place. Apply 3 coats of varnish to all surfaces. Give at least 10 more coats of varnish to the découpaged areas of the chair only. Finish with a coat of matt varnish, followed by an antique wax.

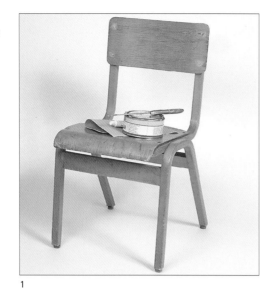

1

2

3

4

5

6

CHILD'S CHAIR

This old school chair is the type you could easily buy very cheaply in a junk shop or garage sale, and the transformation that has been brought about is astonishing. The toy motifs used come from a sheet of gift wrapping paper and the chair has been painted in background shades of blue and red to match. A cream-coloured paint would also look good and provide more of a contrasting background. The blue paint has been sanded back in places to reveal the red paint beneath and gives a naturally worn appearance.

If you want something a bit brighter for a child's room, try using pictures of balloons or cartoon characters against a primary-coloured background.

MATERIALS
Wooden chair
Wood filler
Medium-grade sandpaper
Gift wrapping paper of toys, or other source material
Red paint
Blue paint
Cotton bud
Candle
Clear wax
Antique wax
Basic materials kit (see p. 19)

1 Prime the bed head with acrylic paint and, when it is dry, smooth it back with a fine-grade sandpaper. Then apply 2 coats of the light-green paint.

2 When the background colour is dry, pick out the border with the darker green paint. If you think your technique is not good enough to work freehand, use strips of masking tape to protect the rest of the paintwork.

3 Using manicure scissors and a scalpel, carefully cut out the roses. Start with the internal areas of the wreath first, and then cut around the inside of each and, finally, the outside. Spray the back of each with non-contact adhesive and arrange them on the bed head. When you are happy with the design, remove each, apply paste to the bed head and stick it firmly back, pressing out any air bubbles with your fingertips. Wait 30 minutes and then remove excess paste with a damp sponge and leave it for a further two hours.

4 Apply 10 coats of satin varnish, leaving two hours between coats. Sand back the penultimate coat to give a smooth finish.

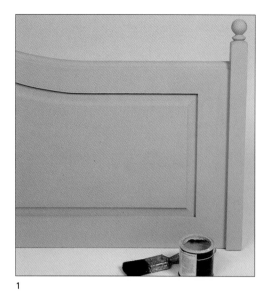

1

2

3

4

MATERIALS

Wooden bed head
Quick-drying acrylic primer
Fine-grade sandpaper
Masking tape
Two shades of green paint
Prints of wreaths of roses, or other source material
Basic materials kit (*see p. 19*)

INTERMEDIATE LEVEL

BED HEAD

This double bed head has been given a fairly formal découpaged design, one that would make it suitable for a bed perhaps in a guest room. If you are decorating the headboard of your own bed, however, you could make the motifs far more personalized – if you like, using a romantically extravagant theme of cherubs and swags.

A child's bed head would obviously require a radically different design approach. This would be an ideal opportunity to involve a child, choosing the motifs to be used together and helping to cut them out and paste them in place. The bed head could be great fun if decorated with such subjects as cartoon and nursery rhyme characters, dinosaurs, cars and so on.

The bed head illustrated above has been painted light green, with the inlaid border picked out in a darker shade, and decorated with wreaths of roses. Shades of blue would look equally good with these motifs and you could use a colour copier to enlarge or reduce the designs so that they fitted your size headboard.

1 The firescreen used in this project is made from medium-density fibreboard (MDF) and, therefore, does not need to be primed or prepared. First, give both sides of the screen 2 coats of the purple paint. Wait for it to dry before proceeding.

2 Run two strips of flexible masking tape adjacent to each other around the edges of the screen, and then remove the outer strip. Rub gilt cream into the space created by the strip of tape you have removed. Masking tape leaves no tacky residue, so this should not cause a problem. Use either your finger or a cotton bud to apply the cream. Wait about 24 hours for the cream to dry.

3 Cut the design out of the sheet of gift wrapping paper, using a pair of sharp manicure scissors and a scalpel knife, and then divide the sheet into six or eight smaller pieces to make it easier to handle. Use the edges of the leaves, flowers and the urn as your dividing lines.

4 Spray the back of each piece of paper with a non-contact adhesive and then reassemble the design on the firescreen. Trim away the incomplete edges of the design so that they fit just inside the gilt border. Paste all the pieces in place, one by one, applying the paste to the screen itself, not the paper. Wait about 30 minutes and then remove excess paste with a damp sponge. Allow at least another two hours before starting to varnish. Apply 10 or 12 coats of varnish, finishing with either a satin or matt coat as required.

1

2

3

4

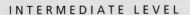

INTERMEDIATE LEVEL

FIRESCREEN

The appealing design for this firescreen came from a single sheet of gift wrapping paper. However, it is always difficult positioning a large piece of paper accurately, and so this one was cut into several smaller pieces and then reassembled on the screen itself.

The shade of purple used for the background colour of the screen is similar to the base colour of the paper, but a light-green shade is also another suitable alternative, depending on the colour of the room it is intended for.

The screen is reversible so you could paste a different design motifs on each side – perhaps using summer and winter decorative themes, for example. A gold gilt border has been applied to finish off the design with a little flair and extravagance.

MATERIALS

Medium-density fibreboard
(MDF) firescreen

Purple paint

sheet of gift wrapping paper,
or other source material

Gilt cream

Cotton bud

Masking tape

Basic materials kit (*see p. 19*)

1 Using coarse-grade sandpaper, remove as much of the lacquer as you can to provide a good base for the paint.

2 Paint all surfaces of the table with a quick-drying acrylic primer and then, when it has dried, with 2 coats of the cream-coloured emulsion. Wait for the paint to dry before proceeding.

3 Carefully cut out the central motif and the borders to fit around the edges of the table, and paste them in position. Always apply paste to the table, not to the back of the prints.

4 Cut out the motifs for the base of the table and paste them into position. Wait about 30 minutes and then remove any excess paste with a damp sponge. When the paste has dried, in about two hours, apply 10 or 12 coats of varnish, leaving two hours between coats. When the varnish is dry, paint on the first, oil-based, coat of the crackle varnish (*see pp. 10-19*). It is best to do this in two stages – the table top and then the table base. Leave this varnish for between two and five hours, depending on room temperature, or until it is just tacky. Then apply the second, water-based, coat so that it completely covers the first. After about half an hour it should be dry and the fine cracks will be visible. Rub the raw umber oil paint, diluted with a little white spirit, into the cracks and wipe off the excess with a piece of kitchen towel. Leave the table for 24 hours and then brush over with a matt-finish, polyurethane oil-based varnish and, when it is dry, apply a coat of antique wax. Wait about 30 minutes and then buff to a mellow shine.

1

2

3

4

CHINESE-INSPIRED TABLE

The table seen opposite was bought very inexpensively from a department store and it was already coated with a mahogany-coloured lacquer. The shape of the table suggested the Chinese pattern motifs, which were taken from a plate design in the British Museum, and the result is a very stylish wine table for a formal dining room.

The central motif was printed on a cream background that matched the colour of the paint used, so careful cutting out was not necessary. However, the border design and the motifs on the legs each had to be cut out individually. As a finishing touch, the table has been given an aged look using a crackle varnish technique (*see pp. 10-19*) and a coat of antique wax.

MATERIALS

Small medium-density
fibreboard (MDF) table

Coarse-grade sandpaper

Quick-drying acrylic primer

Cream-coloured paint

Prints of Chinese motifs,
or other source material

Both parts of crackle varnish
(*see pp. 10-19*)

Raw umber oil paint

White spirit

Oil-based polyurethane varnish

Antique wax

Basic materials kit (*see p. 19*)

BLANKET BOX

This blanket box with its découpaged tulip design has been inspired by New England and Dutch folk art. The clever use of colour photocopies has created laterally reversed mirror-like images, and the flowers were enlarged to achieve an overall balanced design. The quality and capabilities of photocopiers vary considerably and so you may need to experiment until you achieve the effect you want.

The blanket box has been painted in three different shades of blue and the lines around the panels should not look too regular and perfectly rendered. You could use a *trompe l'oeil* technique if you wish, by painting the top and one side a slightly lighter shade than the other. There is space on the lid of the box for a monogram and you could also decorate the side and the back of the chest if you wished, depending on where it is to be positioned in the room.

1 Prime the blanket box with 1 coat of shellac sanding sealer and, when it is dry, apply 2 coats of the medium-blue paint to all surfaces of the box. When the paint is completely dry, lay the box carefully on its side in order to paint its feet (if applicable).

2 Cut a piece of cardboard, or use an appropriate shape such as a table mat, to act as a template, and draw the central panels on the front of the box. Use a ruler to make sure that each panel is evenly placed.

3 Place strips of masking tape around the outside edges of the panel and then paint each one in the light blue colour.

4 When the paint is dry, remove the masking tape. Place fresh strips of tape on the inside of the panels and other strips offset by about ¼in (6mm), leaving a thin, even line between the strips of tape. Fill the gap in with the darkest shade of blue paint and, when it is dry, carefully remove the tape. Paint the borders at the top and bottom of the chest in the same colour.

5 Using a pair of sharp manicure scissors, carefully cut out all the tulip motifs and arrange the

1

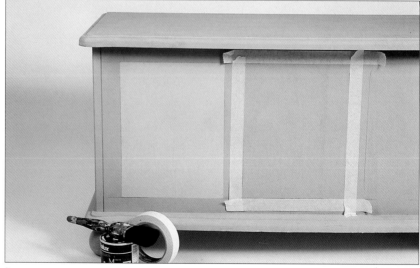
2

3

four smaller ones at each corner of the lid of the box. Apply paste to the lid and stick them down in position. Make sure no air bubbles are trapped beneath.

6 Arrange the flowers on the panels at the front of the box and paste them in position. Wait 30 minutes and then remove any excess paste with a damp sponge. Wait a further two hours before varnishing, and then give the entire chest 2 base coats. Wait for the varnish to dry and then brush the antiquing paint on one surface of the box at a time, wiping of the excess with a clean cloth (*see pp. 10-19*). When this has dried, give the entire chest another coat of varnish. On the lid and front, where the motifs have been positioned, apply at least another 10 coats of varnish, finishing with a matt top coat. Wait at least 24 hours and then rub in a good coat of clear or medium-brown wax and buff to a shine.

4

5

6

INDEX

ACKNOWLEDGEMENTS

THE PUBLISHERS AND AUTHOR WOULD LIKE TO THANK THE
FOLLOWING PEOPLE AND ORGANIZATIONS FOR THEIR GENEROUS HELP
AND SUPPORT IN THE PRODUCTION OF THIS BOOK:

SUPPLIER OF ACCESSORIES AND PROPS

THE DINING ROOM SHOP
62-64 WHITE HART LANE
BARNES
LONDON SW13 OP2
(*Loan of props*)

CASPARI LTD AND DANWAY DESIGNS LTD
(*Donation of papers*)

MAMELOCK PRESS
(*Donation of scraps*)

TEXAS HOMECARE LTD
(*Donation of furniture, pp. 100-101 and 104-109*)

SCUMBLE GOOSE
1 COTSWOLD PLACE
CHALFORD HILL
STROUD
GLOS GL6B8EJ
(*Donation of items, pp. 50-1 and 64-5*)

HOME STALL PRODUCTS
POOL FARM
COUGHTON
ALCESTER
WARKS B49 5HZ
(*Donation of furniture, pp. 102-3*)

SPECIAL THANKS TO

KATHIE GILL FOR INDEXING

SANDRA AND PETER, NICK AND CAROLINE, AND JENNY AND STEWART
FOR THE USE OF THEIR HOMES FOR PHOTOGRAPHY

MIRANDA, ZOË AND KEIRA FOR HELP WITH PAINTING AND CUTTING